# Change Your Perspective Change Your Life

## A Guide For Conscious Living

Gary & Neha Hinebaugh

Copyright © 2025 by Neha & Gary Hinebaugh and Higher Dimensional Guidance & Healing LLC. All rights reserved. This book or any portion thereof may not be reproduced or used in any manner whatsoever without the written permission of the authors, except for the use of quotations with the author's names and book title mentioned. To request permission, send an email to higherdimensionalbooks@gmail.com

ISBN: 979-8-9869088-2-3
Printed in the United States of America

First Printing: January 2025
Library of Congress Number (LCCN): 2024923133
US Copyright: TXu 2-467-194
Cover Design and Layout: Neha Hinebaugh

Disclaimer: Any guidance and information provided in this book is for your thoughtful consideration only. Gary and Neha Hinebaugh and Higher Dimensional Guidance & Healing LLC are not responsible for the reader's interpretation or decisions based on information provided. The reader accepts full personal and legal responsibility for their own life choices.

Published by Higher Dimensional Guidance & Healing LLC
www.higherdimensional.net

## Neha's Gratitude

For Gary, My Love: *Walking this journey with you is the greatest honor of my life. I love you with all the love my heart holds. Thank you!!!*

For Margret, My Mom: *Nothing touches my heart more than being close to you again, trusting, sharing, and laughing together after a lifetime of so much between us. Danke, meine Liebe.*

For The Divine Mother & Father: *In unending gratitude, I give you all my trust, all my love, my hands and feet, my heart, and my voice. Please help me stay true to my Spirit and Divine purpose, always.*

## Gary's Gratitude

For My Divine Partner, My Best Friend, Wife & Office Babe: *So much gratitude, Neha, for all you do and all you are. Without you I could never be me. So much gratitude for you. I couldn't begin to imagine my life without you.*

For My Guides, Angels, Ancestors, Light & Healing Teams And All Others Who Guide Me Through Life: *Thanks for bailing me out over and over.*

For Mother And Father: *I owe you all that I am with so much gratitude. My life would not have this meaning without your guidance, clarity, love, grace, mercy, and compassion. I have all the love I possess for you.*

# Table of Contents

Glossary .................................................................. XII

Foreword ................................................................. XX

Learning To Live ........................................................ 1

Stand Tall In Your Purpose ........................................ 2

From Survival Mode To Thriving ............................... 3

The Language Of Resonance ..................................... 4

Embracing Our Experiences ....................................... 5

Learning To Love Ourselves ....................................... 6

Living From the Heart ............................................... 7

The Crack Is Where The Light Comes In .................... 8

Experiencing Without Judgement .............................. 9

You Are Sacred ........................................................ 10

The Will Power Needed To Make Life Changes ........ 11

Honoring The Boundaries of Others ......................... 13

The Block Of Perception .......................................... 14

To The Conscious Men ............................................ 15

Healing Our Fears Of Abandonment ........................ 17

Evolving Beyond Our Darkness ................................ 18

We Are Limitless Beings .......................................... 19

Your Relationship With Yourself .............................. 20

Respecting Our Healing Journey .............................. 21

Coming Out Of Survival Mode ................................. 22

How To Make It Through Volatile Times .................. 23

You Owe No Loyalty To Your Ancestor's Limitations ..... 24
Going Into Our Darkness ................................................. 25
Gratitude For Who We Were In The Past ..................... 27
Teach The Children Well ................................................ 28
Connecting With Mother/Father God .......................... 29
Happy At Heart ................................................................30
Overcoming Near Impossible Odds .............................. 31
Finding Beauty In The Darkness ................................... 32
The Inward Journey Of Awakening ............................... 33
Getting To Know Your Self ............................................ 34
The Importance of Trusting Our Guides ...................... 35
We Are Not Failing ......................................................... 39
Willingness To Change ................................................... 40
Living In the Present ...................................................... 41
Gratitude At the End of the Day ................................... 42
Surrendering Our Need For Control ............................ 43
Personal Boundaries ....................................................... 44
Nurturing Our Body Back To Health .......................... 45
The Rewarding Journey of Deep Healing ..................... 47
The Demand For Abundance ........................................ 48
The Vulnerability of Evolution ...................................... 49
Live and Let Live ............................................................. 50
Practicing Discernment During These Times .............. 51
Advice From My Spirit To My Younger Selves ............ 52
Embracing Our Darkness ............................................... 53

Living In Our Natural State ................................................. 55
How Our Guides Help Us with Our Healing ..................... 56
Keeping Up With Our Internal Changes ........................... 58
Overcoming Our Need To Control Everything ................. 59
The Medicine of Trust ..................................................... 60
Lowering Our Walls ......................................................... 61
A Different Perspective on Being Triggered ..................... 62
Raising Your Vibration .................................................... 63
Living From The Heart .................................................... 64
There Is Always Another Way .......................................... 65
The Unhealed Spiritual Ego ............................................. 66
Divine Sovereignty .......................................................... 67
The Inner Child Is Our Connection To The Divine .......... 69
Planting Seeds Of Light For The Future .......................... 70
Living Life On Life's Terms ............................................. 71
Letting Go Of The Old .................................................... 72
Facing Our Traumas ........................................................ 73
Overcoming Our Fears .................................................... 74
Being in Judgement Of Others ........................................ 75
What To Do When We Are Triggered .............................. 76
Learning From Those We Encounter ............................... 77
Building A New Foundation For The Future ................... 78
Doing What We Came Here To Do .................................. 79
Why We Shy Away From Making Changes ..................... 80
Opinions Are The Lowest Form Of Knowledge ................ 81

Working With Traumatic Memories ........................... 82
The Natural Process Of Deep Healing ......................... 83
Our Trust Has To Be Earned ..................................... 86
Gratitude For Learning Our Lessons .......................... 87
The Fruits Of Our Inner Work ................................... 87
The Gifts of Vulnerability ......................................... 88
Healing Our Inner Child ........................................... 89
The Basis For Our Relationships ................................ 90
Learning To Like Ourselves Again ............................. 91
Letting Go Of Expectations ...................................... 93
The Bridge Will Appear ........................................... 94
Creating New References As We Evolve ..................... 95
Going Within ......................................................... 96
The Celestial Consciousness Of Mother Earth ............. 97
Don't Force Your Healing ......................................... 99
From Self-Loathing To Self-Love ............................. 100
Staying True To Our Journey .................................. 101
Healing Hurtful Projections from Childhood ............. 102
The Necessity For Humility .................................... 103
Setting Healthy Boundaries .................................... 104
Preserving Our Sovereignty In Love Relationships ..... 105
Revisiting Our Experiences in Gratitude ................... 108
Forgiving Ourselves For Hurting Others ................... 109
Finding Our Own Truth ......................................... 110
When The Universe Closes Doors On Us ................. 111

Let Life Touch You ............................................................ 112
When It's Time To Let People Go .............................. 113
Opportunity To Learn, Grow, and Heal ...................... 114
The Promise Of A New Way, A New Day .................... 115
Without Trust There Can Be No Evolution ................. 116
The Ride Of Our Lives .............................................. 117
Labor Of Love ........................................................ 118
People Come And Go In Our Lives ........................... 119
We Are Never Finished ........................................... 120
The Hardships That Drive Our Evolution .................. 121
Taking Steps Toward Our Dreams ............................ 122
Spiritual Wake-Up Call ............................................ 123
The Roller Coaster Ride Of Life ............................... 124
Harm No One ....................................................... 125
Breathe Before You Act .......................................... 126
The Adventure Of Our Life ..................................... 127
The Evolution Of Our Spirit .................................... 128
No More Self-Sacrificing ......................................... 129
There Is Magic In The Unknown ............................. 130
Let Your Healing Be Organic ................................... 131
Seeing Truth When The Timing Is Right ................... 132
The Value Of Being In The Moment ........................ 133
Blaming The Divine ............................................... 134
Trust Is All We Have ............................................... 135
Facing Ourselves .................................................... 136

Keeping Our Past Out Of The Present .......................... 137
Seeing Truth ............................................................ 138
Self-Care During Difficult Times ................................ 139
The Gift Of Trust ..................................................... 141
Healing Our Ancestral Lineage ................................... 142
Transitional Phases On Our Journey ............................ 143
Phoenix Out Of The Ashes ......................................... 144
We Are Not Who We Have Become ............................ 145
Learning Grace ........................................................ 146
Honesty About Our Own Toxic Behaviors .................... 147
The Purposes Of Our Incarnation ................................ 150
Moving On From Our Traumas ................................... 151
The Process of Internal Checks And Balances ................ 152
Rising Beyond our Yesterdays ..................................... 153
Our Loved Ones In The Etheric .................................. 154
Facing Our Own Mortality ......................................... 155
Experiencing and Feeling Deeply ................................ 156
The Pitfalls Of Channeling And Psychic Readings ........... 157
Creating New Reference Points ................................... 159
The Process Of Changing Our Mindset ........................ 160
Feeling Our Emotions Fully ....................................... 161
Balance And The Aquarian Age .................................. 162
Making Your Stand .................................................. 163
Our Divine Heritage ................................................. 164
The Dangers of the Bliss Bunny Syndrome .................... 165

The Importance Of Internal Boundaries ........................ 167
Finding The Strength To Go On ................................. 168
Allowing Our Relationships To Change ........................ 169
There Can Be No Evolution Without Trust .................... 171
Trusting The Processes Of Healing ............................. 172
The Balance Of Dark And Light ................................. 173
Believing In Yourself Again ....................................... 174
Bringing Change For Future Generations ..................... 175
Our Birthright Of Freedom ........................................ 176
The True Power Of The Enabler ................................. 177
Finding Your Courage .............................................. 178
Self-Forgiveness For What Was Done To Us .................. 179
Learning To Receive ................................................ 182
Living In Grace ....................................................... 183
Doing What We Must ............................................... 184
You Are A Limitless Being ......................................... 185
Stepping Out Of The Box .......................................... 186
Making Ourselves The Priority In Our Life ................... 187
Learning Healthy External Boundaries ......................... 190
Safely Releasing Our Emotions ................................... 191
The Damaging Effect Of Projections ............................ 192
Learning Discernment of Energies .............................. 193
Don't Lower Your Energy For Others .......................... 194
From The Ashes Of The Old ...................................... 195
Knowing Your Own Energy Signature ......................... 196

Taking Time for Yourself ............................................. 197
Going Within For Our Answers ................................. 198
Collateral Beauty ......................................................... 199
Shift Your Perspective ................................................ 200
Expanding Into The Unknown ................................. 201
The Futility Of Forcing Our Agenda ........................ 202
Coming Out Of Victim Mode ................................... 203
When Others Bring Drama Into Our Lives ............. 204
Revisiting Old Wounds ............................................... 205
Allowing Changes In Our Relationships .................. 206
The Right To Choose ................................................. 207
Actions Speak Louder Than Words .......................... 208
Honoring Another's Truth ......................................... 209
Embracing our Emotions ........................................... 210
Unlearning Perfectionism ........................................... 211
Being The Observer .................................................... 212
Moving On From The Past ........................................ 213
Balancing Our Darkness ............................................. 214
Don't Ever Lose Hope ................................................ 215
Cleansing Your Space .................................................. 218
Experiencing Beyond Our Survival Mode ............... 219
Our Internal Dance Of Light And Dark .................. 220
Gary's Book: An Awakening Perspective ................. 221

# Glossary

This section offers clarification and definitions to some of the terms that are used in this book, not from a dictionary, but from our own understanding and the context in which we use them.

**Akashic Records** The Akashic Records, or simply the Akash, is a compilation of every soul's journey throughout time, past, present, and future. It contains every thought, word, deed of every soul. There is no judgement held within these pages, therefore no punishment. When we transition back to the Spirit after our lifetime, we read our own record to see how we performed against what we contracted for in this lifetime. We sit in assessment of ourselves, learning what we will make right in our next incarnation and what we achieved, but without punishment. Some intuitives and psychics access the Akash and its wisdom and knowledge to be shared with others. We stand within no right or wrong in the reading of our Akashic Record, simply gain an understanding of how we fared against the contracts we signed before our incarnation.

**Authentic Self or Spirit Self** Our authentic self is defined as our Spirit and not our 3D (3-dimensional) self. Who we are authentically is different from who we have become through our lifetime here. To achieve authenticity is to unbecome who we have been molded to be through the projections and conditioning of others, and every institution of learning. To become authentic again, begins by going back to our childhood, unlearning who we have been taught to be. This process will change outdated, stifling patterns and beliefs, and replace them with our own, meant for our highest good. We are then, as we did when we were young children, embodying the true, loving nature of our Spirit self, our Divine self in the higher dimensions. This process to our authenticity will be completed upon our transition back to the Spirit world when our vessel expires.

**Awakening** To awaken means to be consciously aware of the self, while existing in the moment and experiencing it without judgement. We are allowing life to happen organically, living every aspect of our lives from the heart, and connecting to our own Divinity through becoming our authentic limitless selves... our Spirit. This means that we are maintaining our 3D existence and existing in another dimension as our Spirit selves simultaneously.

**Beings** All beings are sentient because they have a Spirit and soul (the incarnated part of the Spirit). They are sentient because they have a conscience with awareness. The term Beings also includes all intergalactic and higher dimensional entities, most of whom are more evolved than humans existing on this Earth, as well as our furry friends, who are also more advanced than us in many ways.

**Collective Consciousness** Every being throughout the multiverse is connected by an invisible string to the Divine, therefore inseparable. We all come from the same source and are a part of each other, yet unique. We share a common journey, while on our own personal journeys, contributing to the evolution of all beings through our personal and shared experiences. Every being and their journey are unique to their purposes of existence, contracted before any incarnation and carried over from lifetime to lifetime.

**Comfort Zone** Throughout our lives, we create little boxes of comfort, allowing us to live within familiar limitations and feel safe. We live strictly within this comfort zone, believing our lives to be good and proper, and easily navigated. Unfortunately, we can neither grow nor evolve within our comfort zone, and remain locked in status quo, unable to move forward. Anything outside of this, and we feel vulnerable, not knowing how to proceed within the discomfort of our vulnerability and without our familiar limitations.

**Dark Night of the Soul** This is a process of transformation. Its purpose is to facilitate our conscious journey through a phase of extremely deep emotional healing to bring us back to the Spirit self and out of being stuck in our 3D existence. This transformation can be quite painful as the Universe forces us to face our own darkness to bring light in quantum measure. This will last as long as necessary to bring us to where we need to be on our Divine path that has been neglected by the 3D self. When this process has been completed, our perceptions are aligned with our Spirit self, seeing a higher truth, and our existence becomes higher dimensional.

**Divinity or Divine** We refer to what is commonly known as God or Source, which is actually pure consciousness energy without form. We all come from this Source Consciousness, which is within us all. The recognition of our own inner Divinity is the awareness and acceptance of this energy within the self. Our connection to the Divine is our Spirit self. We all are sovereign Beings within Divinity, unique to our journey within the Collective Consciousness, and a part of each other.

**Divine Sovereignty** Every sentient being/every Spirit has the Divinely given right to their own inherent authenticity. This means that we do not owe our lives to any outside influence. We are free to choose, and live our lives according to our own nature and choices, as long as we harm no one. Many of us are now rediscovering our authenticity and reclaiming our Divine Sovereignty, after having been conditioned and molded according to who the world around us wanted us to be. This means that we are taking ownership of our lives and learning to live in accordance with who we truly are. (This is a spiritual definition and not a religious one.)

**Evolution** From a spiritual and conscious awareness perspective, evolution is a constant change, transformation, and transition from one state of consciousness to a higher state of being. Since change is the only constant on our spiritual journey, we can't help but to evolve. We come into this world with no tools for our earthly existence. As we age, we collect tools that help us grow, physically and spiritually. With conscious awareness, we find opportunities to learn, heal, and grow, expanding every aspect of our lives to step into the next phase. Transitioning from one phase to the next higher phase brings us evolution, from our very beginnings to our eventual transition back to the Spirit as we exit our 3D vessel. The same goes for beings of light and darkness alike, even though we are all born of the light. There are those who evolve into darkness, choosing a path without love.

**Higher Dimensional** The higher dimensions exist within the self beyond the mundane 3D life, and are not a location in the cosmos with form. A higher dimensional existence expresses evolution beyond what we currently know and accept, where the Spirit self is found. It transcends the ego-driven life with acceptance and trust, facilitating a heart-based existence through unconditional love and recognition of our Inner Divinity. We are living life as our authentic limitless self, from the heart in every aspect. The only way to the higher dimensions is through our true authenticity, existing as the Spirit self.

**Mindset** We have a choice to live beyond our current truths and beliefs to bring change out of the status quo of our comfort zone. With awareness and recognition we are able to evolve. A change in mindset is moving above our current thought processes, permitting old patterns and beliefs to be replaced. We are allowing ourselves to be authentic, transcending our current self-imposed limitations, and bringing evolution in profound measure. This change enables us to see more possibilities, unlocking untapped potential to rise above our current state of existence.

**Sacred or Divine Feminine** During thousands of years of patriarchal rule, the feminine principle was almost completely buried underneath intentional distortions, lies, and perversions. As humanity is shifting out of the colonizations of the Piscean Age and into the balance and personal freedoms of the Aquarian Age, the feminine principles of compassion, intuition, nurturing love, creativity, receptivity, and equanimity are crucial for the survival of our species and our planet. The Sacred Feminine is a universal energy, rather than a gender-oriented concept. At the highest level, the Divine Feminine is represented by the Source Consciousness of the Divine Mother, whom humanity also had forgotten in their focus on masculine power. We have entered an age where women and men alike are learning to balance their inherent internal energies, honoring the Sacred Feminine as well as the Sacred Masculine principles, which is truly the way to overcome the pains of duality, finding inner peace and wholeness.

**Soul Contracts** A soul contract maps our whole life from beginning to end. Before we incarnate into any lifetime, much time is spent with other souls in agreement, outlining every aspect of our lives. Necessary things such as our name, date and time of birth, date and time of expiration, our parents, siblings, friends, and partners… are made in advance of our incarnation. Every experience, situation, core belief, physical appearance, and our role in this lifetime are meant for our highest good and evolution. We are given opportunities to learn, grow, and heal through challenges, and free will for our Spirit to choose what is for our highest good. Some believe these contracts can be changed and even broken, should they not be in our best interests. It's crucial to remember that other souls have free will within our shared journeys. This is where life becomes complicated, as we don't always know how their choices will affect our journey, and vice versa.

**Shift or Universal Shift** The shift or Universal shift we have been waiting for is upon us. It is a noted transition within humankind from unawareness to conscious awareness, with a connectedness to our own inner Divinity. It is being facilitated by Earth entering the Age of Aquarius, the balancing of masculine and feminine energies, and out of the Piscean Age of harsh patriarchal rule. It is in response to the current global decline of core values back to spiritual needs and sustainable living in the context of spirituality. It is meant for our spiritual evolution and the evolution of Earth, necessary for the betterment of our galaxy and its inhabitants.

**Spirituality** Our spiritual journey is a means of living beyond the accepted 3D limitations and identity, and is of the Spirit, not the material world. In actuality, it is living a life as our authentic limitless self in a heart-based existence, moving away from the limitations and constructs of the 3D, inward toward the higher dimensions. It's knowing that life is not about our material wants and desires, rather the acceptance of our Inner Divinity and allowing our Spirit self to guide us beyond an ego-based reality.

**Vulnerability** As we step outside of our familiar comfort zone, we encounter that incredibly uncomfortable feeling where we are raw and open to the unknown. We are allowing ourselves to expand and evolve with trust, while letting go of the illusion that we can control life. Being vulnerable, we accept change and not knowing our direction or what comes next. We are learning to trust and believe in ourselves, and our journey to authenticity, allowing life to be as it's meant to be, not how we believe it should be. Our vulnerability is the only state of being within which we can learn, grow, and heal, as we break the illusions we have created through perceptions guided by our wounded ego.

# Foreword

Do you realize in several hundred years, this very time will be looked upon with much interest? Take a look back several hundred years to a much different time and place. The here and now is the basis for the future of humanity. We are setting the new way of life for all of mankind. During our lifetime has been much recognition of a different way of existing. Yes, it's volatile, yes, it's dark. But we are bringing the much-needed light to prominence, and a different understanding of life in general.

We have begun to change ancestral patterns of being. We are living much more from the heart than was experienced several hundred years ago. We are bringing a new inner landscape to life. We are breaking old patterns and beliefs, making way for an even more balanced way of living. This is the foundation of the New Way, the New Day brought to light by Yeshu by learning to live from the heart. We are embracing a personal freedom that has been kept in darkness by millennia of patriarchal rule.

With the Age of Aquarius in full swing, we're learning how to balance our masculine and feminine energies within, at a pace never before experienced. There will, someday, be an event horizon bringing the majority of humanity into this balanced lifestyle. More freedoms will be available and accepted because of our silent revolution here, right now. We're raising the bar for a higher standard of living our personal lives, in peace and with love in our hearts.

As we move through these historically unprecedented times, with a front row seat to the crumbling of our civilization, we will be tempted to get stuck in the heartbreak of what is happening on our planet. It is important to give ourselves time to grieve, and as soon as we can connect with our Spirit, and be the beacon of light that we truly are – for ourselves and those around us.

The burden of the world does not belong on our shoulders. We can have compassion, but we cannot take on what is not ours to carry. This would only be self-destructive and keep us from doing what we came here to do in this lifetime. Boundaries within ourselves and with the outer world are incredibly important right now to protect ourselves from getting sucked into battles that are not our own.

There is a larger picture available regarding this phase of planetary transformation that includes the healing and ascension of Mother Earth and the evolution of our human species. Many of us are here to be midwives to this process. We are truly a part of a massive support net - on and around our planet - that includes many millions of bright, loving beings in the higher dimensions who support our every effort.

At an individual level, many of us are guided to do deep inner work, heal our past traumas, and change the transgenerational patterns that were projected onto us. With everything that is going on, our nervous systems are frazzled. We are trying to stay out of the way of other people's craziness and find some semblance of balance and peace within ourselves.

In order to bring the change we want to see in the world, we have to be the change. We have to embody the new, and live and breathe it, not just talk about it. We have to allow ourselves to be transformed into who we are meant to be according to our Spirit, and let the waves of change wash away all that no longer serves our highest good. Along the way, we have to learn trust in ourselves and the Divine, so that we can build a new foundation for living, within ourselves, based on original authenticity and not societal conditioning.

Our healing efforts are going quantum right now, being met with great support from the higher dimensions. We are certainly not alone as we personally and collectively go through this intense metamorphosis. There are many millions of us on parallel journeys. Acceptance and willingness are key to finding a new normal at a higher frequency, while embracing the often uncomfortable unfoldment of the unknown. As we are rapidly changing, we often don't know ourselves anymore and feel lost. We are urged to find comfort in the love that we carry in our hearts and offer it to ourselves. There are purposes beyond our limited understanding. We are called to trust ourselves and the Divine, and allow our minds to open. We were made for this time.

We hope that the words in this book and the energy between the lines may touch the depth of your heart, activate a new understanding, and help you access the love and inner wisdom that your Spirit already possesses. We offer these words humbly from our hearts to yours, hoping that they may help you change your perspective, see your true worth, and embrace the fullness of the life that is yours to live, as it is meant to be.

The only recommendation we give is to read slowly. This is not a book to be read in a day or a week, and then set aside. Read a bit and let it marinate. Give yourself time to truly absorb the words. Bookmark the sections that touch you and read them again. We are deeply honored that you are holding this book in your hands.

> *"Learning is freedom.*
> *Learning is much faster if you see it*
> *as the way to your freedom.*
> *You are building a new foundation."*

# Learning To Live

To fully be alive with every fiber of our being means to not control life, but to ride the wave of the moment with allowance and surrender, with trust, and with gratitude. It means to be open to experiencing what the moment brings, regardless of our preference not to feel pain, not to get dirty, and not to live this messy life to a heartbreaking depth. Our need for control does not save us, nor does it shield us from life's devastations. It only gives the illusion that we can change reality by manipulating our perception. Slowly, we are learning to trust instead of panic. To stay and breathe instead of plotting our escape. To be fully present and observe, instead of trying to control everything around us in such a manner that we can feel safe. We are learning to come home to ourselves, pouring love and compassion into our wounds and fears, and embracing the naked godly child that lives within our heart.

## Stand Tall In Your Purpose

Every conscious decision we make, everything we do for our highest good doesn't end with us. Our free will to choose a higher path adds to the Collective free will. It's coming into the Collective in balance, as we all come from the light. Every experience, every thought, word, and deed is streaming throughout life itself. Your decision to choose a journey of light and living in a state of love is so very important during this time and for decades to come. This is one major way in which we all are building the new foundation for the future of humanity and Mother Gaia. When we don't use our free will for our highest good, we also send this to the Collective free will. Many of us are not aware of this fact and some of us may need to adjust our use of free will. We're fighting for the future of our children, grandchildren, and our family line for generations to come. Stand tall in your purpose and choose to live from the heart. The future is counting on us, and we all need to buckle down and stay true to the contracts we signed before we incarnated here. This is how we change the world - one being at a time.

# From Survival Mode To Thriving

Most of humanity has never been able to step out of survival mode. Something happened in our lives, usually in early childhood, which activated heavy trauma responses within the self. Our emotions shut down and we instinctively dissociated the traumatic memories, learning to live over top of them. As we grew, our tense state of inner division grew with us, becoming more solidified and shrouded in unawareness. Repressed memories and emotions may have surfaced as we progressed on our journey. Yet, most of us have never been able to step outside of the survival mechanisms that once arose in an attempt to protect ourselves from breaking. The underlying need to control every aspect of our lives and that of others, our self-centeredness, and need to play god, the inability to go within… all indicate that we are stuck in survival mode. Now is the time to learn to truly live - rather than just survive. You have the power to change the patterns that have kept you bound and unhappy. The wholeness and aliveness that you have been seeking in the outer world will be restored to you as you do the inner work. Open your heart and allow yourself to trust and believe in yourself again. You are safe now. Allow the changes.

# The Language Of Resonance

We are learning the language of resonance which goes hand in hand with trusting ourselves. Every day we are faced with a multitude of situations that require our choice, response, or action in some form. We are learning to listen to our inner guidance, our Spirit, and guides in the higher dimensions, trying to determine the best response or course of action in any given moment. When we pay attention to resonance, we know without a doubt what we need to do. It is not necessary to use a pendulum or do muscle testing as a gauge that can be manipulated or controlled by the mind. We have the sensing mechanism already built into our being. All it takes is to allow ourselves to be shown where the resonance lies, where the deeper connection is truly felt. We are learning to build trust within the self again, and this is a part of the new foundation for living from the heart that we are building - to be in touch with our own knowing, our higher guidance system. Listen and feel deeply and practice trusting yourself.

# Embracing Our Experiences

All that we experience is a part of our journey. Not judging our experiences makes them an integral necessity, regardless of how we perceive them. All of our experiences are neutral. We give them definition as to being bad, good, indifferent, or just plain ugly. Please understand, they all were necessary according to the contracts that we signed before our incarnation. Without the need to project our perception onto our experiences, we can clearly see the truth of their offerings and what they brought to us. If our lives were filled with nothing but a perceived good, would we have the gift of balance in our lives? This balance affords us opportunities for growth, healing, and learning, ensuring our evolution as it's meant to be. It also shows us the ability to expand simply by seeing them as a gift, not a curse. I truly believe that our perception can and will change the course of our journeys. Experiences were never intended to punish us, rather they bring insight into ourselves, strictly by our reaction or response. Learning to respond, rather than react gives us space to evaluate our position, whereas our reaction will mainly come from our woundedness. See the experience as the observer, not from the woundedness, and the truth will manifest itself and not our judgement.

# Learning To Love Ourselves

Deep down and underneath it all, most of us have never felt good about ourselves. The shaming of our childhood still festers in our bones, and distorts our perception of ourselves. We silently judge ourselves so harshly, measuring ourselves against some unattainable standard of perfectionism that no human being could actually ever achieve. And we dislike and reject ourselves still, because the people in our lives, from whom we wanted love and approval the most, could not see us and could not love us – not because we were unlovable but because they were so traumatized. If you really stop and look at yourself, at who you have become despite everything that you have been through, can you see how unfair your self-condemnation is, and how wrong you are in the firm belief that you are not good enough? Your woundedness goes deep, but so does your strength, courage, and the beauty of your heart. Heal your relationship with yourself, and give yourself the love and approval that you have yearned for all your life.

## Living From the Heart

Open your heart to see what is unseen. The seat of love is within. Look not with your eyes. Hear what your ears cannot. Through the love in your heart, is where the mysteries of life are discovered. Only through the trust in the Divine can one begin to see truth. We have an existence far beyond the 3D world in which we live. This is where truth can be found. Within. The outer world has nothing for us outside of its reality. We did not create this reality from the depths of our pain. We do not create outside of our own existence. We can only create the world in which we exist; within. The outer world was created by the woundedness of others and has nothing to do with those on a journey of the Light. This is not our reality. Our reality is formed within the love of our hearts, not by those filled with anger and hatred. That is their reality, not ours. Be true to you and remain true to your journey and the purposes that you are called to fulfill, or not… That is for you to choose. But I will say this… live from the heart and the love meant for you will be returned. There is no greater bounty than knowing we have lived from the heart in every aspect of our lives. This is not the purpose of all, but in your world, it is all that matters. Love is all that matters. This is our natural state. Be that. God loves you and so do I.

# The Crack Is Where The Light Comes In

Everyday being on this planet is a miracle. The heaviness of the atmosphere itself makes it hard to exist here. Duality is very pronounced, and the cycle of life and death very prominent. Battles are the norm. And together, at this time, we are witnessing the most extraordinary historic occurrence. Our human species, along with the celestial consciousness of Mother Earth, is undergoing a massive shift, an evolutionary quantum leap into a new dimension of existence. As humans, we are so glued to our comfort zone and our survival defenses that, unfortunately, we often have to be confronted with extreme circumstances and emotions in order to be shaken out of our slumber and wake up. We experience disasters, personal losses, the upheaval of our life and everything that was familiar and defined us. When we are forced to let go and to surrender because we have nothing else left, an openness is created within us - a crack where the light comes in. We are suddenly much more connected to our Spirit and our guides. Ripped open with such violence and abruptness, we have suddenly been slam-dunked back home. Our hearts flung open the moment our world came crashing down on us.

# Experiencing Without Judgement

Adversity is a fact of life we cannot escape, no matter how much we try to control our lives, so how do we overcome it when bad things happen? We need to accept that it has happened, first off, and the rest is how we respond and react to the experience as this will set in motion everything that follows. We can either choose to be a victim to it, and be stuck in asking why, or we can see the experience as an opportunity to learn, heal, and grow but we need to allow the experience without judgment. Changing our perspective of any situation or experience gives us the freedom of choosing what happens next and the ability to change ourselves and our lives. Instead of seeing an obstacle, change your perception to seeing opportunity to further your evolution. Look beyond your perceived pain and heartache, and see what you can build upon to make changes within yourself. How much we suffer is a choice we consciously make if we choose to remain a victim. See the truth of the experience and the lessons that the Universe has brought, and you will see within yourself room to heal, learn, and grow. That choice is going to make the difference in your life.

## You Are Sacred

It is all sacred… The parts of ourselves that we reject and do not like. All that we cannot accept about ourselves. Our mistakes and misperceptions. Our guilt and shame. All that we are learning through the hard lessons of life. Our daily struggle to heal and change old patterns. Our attempts to not project our anger and desperation onto those around us. Our kindness and hope to change the world… We make ourselves so small and think so little of ourselves. Or go to the other extreme and build a pedestal for ourselves to comfort our sense of being unworthy. We place expectations of perfection on ourselves, and shame ourselves for falling short. We have stopped trusting ourselves and the Universe so long ago that we cannot remember how not to live locked into survival mode. It's all sacred… We do not have the right to put ourselves down and dismiss who we are. We are indeed sacred. With all parts and all that we are – our inherent Divinity as much as our body, ego, inner child, and our human experience. Embrace yourself and give yourself the love and respect that you deserve. You are sacred.

# The Will Power Needed To Make Life Changes

Change does not come until we are a hundred percent willing to do what it takes to bring about the life changes needed. We may have worked our way up to being ninety-seven percent ready to implement what needs to be done. A lot of work has gone into coming to this point, including coming up with the courage and allowance for breaking the related old habits. But that last little bit of not wanting to leave our comfort zone will keep us stuck, even if we can no longer tolerate our current circumstances, and have truly had enough of our suffering. Holding on to that last little bit of self-sabotage or self-punishment will keep us from moving forward. Often, we have to hit a rock bottom before we can let go. At this point, we need to change so desperately that we are allowing a surrender to the Divine, to whatever degree we can. In that moment, we have let go of needing to have things our way, and are truly willing to do whatever it takes. At the threshold of the door that we must walk through, we are stripped of our previous control. For us to truly be able to make the changes necessary and move forward, we must be a thousand percent dedicated and give to it with every fiber of our being, no matter the cost. A level of dedication is needed that unearths a storm surge inside, of sheer willpower. At the point where we will, under no circumstances, still accept the old ways or the current painful circumstances, we will have broken open that door to a new way of being. Where the changes we initiated will actually land is not under our control, as we are embedded in a web of connectivity all around us, seen and unseen. The new will be brought to us in the form that it is meant to, as per our Spirit. We have provided the opening for change, which is an enormous accomplishment in itself, given how hard it is to actually get the cellular self to allow a disruption of its status quo. Now, we must trust, implicitly, that the Universe is moving us to where we need to be, allowing the continuation of necessary internal changes, and the arrival of the new ways and freedoms that are meant for us.

# Honoring The Boundaries of Others

No matter how hard we try to do what's right, live a life worthy of our soul contracts and try to find balance, we still have the ability to be toxic to others. What's truly hard sometimes is to understand and be aware of the fact that we are not where others are on their journey. It doesn't place us above or below them, nor does it make us better or less than them. It simply means that we all are in different places on our journey. This is another one of the fine lines we walk on our awakening Journey. It's imperative for us to be aware of the unknown boundaries of others. We can learn those boundaries and abide by them. Just because something works for us and is good for us, doesn't mean that it will work for or is good for others. One of the hardest lessons I have been learning on my journey is to allow others to be who they are, and allow them their journey on their terms. We all have a different understanding, and we all need to remember this fact. The seeds of our knowledge and wisdom can be toxic to others when we are in different places. Sometimes it's best to allow lessons to be learned as they need to be learned.

# The Block Of Perception

All too often, we have a sense of being stuck, unable to move forward. Somewhere within us, just beyond our grasp, is a block, impeding our forward and upward movement. It's important to remember we are always exactly where we are meant to be on our journey. It's our perception that is the block. It's telling us something is wrong, and we begin to have doubt and fear. In reality, we have just created an experience for ourselves that didn't exist or need to happen. As a rule of thumb, we should always doubt our doubts. Becoming the observer allows us to see beyond our own thoughts, beliefs, and judgments, bringing truth and not our vision of events. We become the observer by allowing our Spirit to guide us, and not seeing with our physical eyes, or listening with our physical ears. We instead listen and see with our open heart. Learning to have awareness and recognition of our emotional thoughts is a very necessary step in our healing process, and a huge part of self-mastery. All of these processes are worthy of our acceptance to move forward on our awakening journey - inward toward the Divine self and the higher dimensions.

## To The Conscious Men

To the conscious men: an apology from the conscious women... for stifling your growth as much as we have encouraged it. For dumping our hatred of men onto you, and not seeing you but only our fathers. For controlling and shaming you in the way our mothers taught us. For making you feel guilty for being a man because of eons of patriarchal abuse, not because of you. To the gentle men of kind hearts: we justified our own toxic behavior under the excuse of victimhood. We elevated ourselves above you, maybe through a goddess identity or feminist exclusiveness, to make ourselves feel special and powerful. Please forgive us, as we, too, are learning to be accountable for our thoughts and actions, and how not to project our triggered emotions onto you, but to face and heal them within ourselves.

Through the atrocities done to us by men - other men, not you... we had become so masculine in our prolonged survival mode, our hearts so hardened, and our minds so self-absorbed that we could not see you, and your own daily struggles to free yourself from your own conditioning and not become the kind of man your dad was. The moments when you hesitate and just stand there because you don't want to overstep any boundaries in women, ever. The love that goes into empowering us to be untamed and authentic, to embrace our emotions, to stand our ground with conviction. The time you said to another man, of the outdated kind, that we are not a "girl" and to address us with respect... It is you that we are learning boundaries from and how to speak with natural authority. How to come out of our codependent behaviors and like ourselves so much that we can finally stop seeking approval from others, especially men.

We need you. And we are certainly not above you. That would only switch the roles. A senseless game of trying to make ourselves feel better by doing to you what was done to us. And yet it has been given to us, together, to build the new world and become living demonstrations of a new balance of the feminine and masculine energies.

If we must define ourselves as goddesses, then you may claim to be gods. By our side, not above or below. Together, grounded in reality, honesty, and respect, and in our own divinity. Grounded, for the first time in history on a larger scale, in love. To the conscious men: we see you and we thank you from the bottom of our hearts. We may, indeed, achieve our dreams and thrive as a human species, if we can work together, empower all beings regardless of gender, and in our joining be the bridge to the new world.

# Healing Our Fears Of Abandonment

God has not abandoned us in this crisis. But when we are triggered into fear and survival mode, we temporarily lose awareness of our inherent connectedness, and often feel as though we have been abandoned. Our perception has narrowed to our own safety and comfort. Unable to see beyond our own fear of the future, we take ourselves out of the present moment, and lose access to our intuition and wisdom. Worry is a fear-based response to a situation or experience, often triggered by an unhealed emotional fear or trauma from our past. The root cause of worry is an inability to trust. Worry lowers our vibration, and manifests a toxic chemical imbalance within our body that often results in physical illness. When we believe that we can control life and manipulate the issue we are scared about, our wounded ego is responding to the situation, blocking the flow of life, and increasing our feelings of being disconnected and helpless. Neither worry nor control have ever contributed to our safety or wellbeing. Acceptance, compassion, and trust will bring much better results. We have to remember everything happens as it is meant to when it is meant to. Our free will, response, and reaction will set in motion what happens next. We must remember God does not abandon us - ever. But at times we forget that God is always there for us.

## Evolving Beyond Our Darkness

Have you ever noticed how the darkness at night distorts our perception of truth? We lose the ability for spatial awareness, and really can't determine distance as we can in the daytime light. Our darkness within is exactly the same. We lose the ability to see truth as it is. Oftentimes it brings emotional pain, which distorts the reality of what we are enduring. So, how do we see truth when the darkness impairs and clouds our perception? We close down the 3D ability of all our senses. In other words, we allow the Spirit to see for us. Our woundedness can be the biggest block we must overcome, which is led by our ego-self. This is how we become the observer. The Spirit will always show us truth in reality, as the ego shows us only a distorted observation. This is why we need to let go of the constructs and limitations of the 3D in order to become the authentic being we truly are. Since the Spirit is limitless, it makes sense to allow it to guide us rather than the woundedness we've become accustomed to. This is also an amazing tool for stepping out of the comfort zone we constructed for ourselves many years ago. This vulnerability is so very important, as it is the only state of being in which we can learn, heal, and grow. This means allowing the necessary changes within. Let go of the 3D control and allow your Spirit to guide you. It takes less energy, which you can use in better ways for your evolution.

## We Are Limitless Beings

How can we know what our untapped potential is, if we don't allow ourselves access to it? The comfort zone we have created for ourselves is actually stifling us, through the limitations we have set and chosen to live within. We are limitless beings undefined and unbound by the 3D and its constructs. There is one sure path to becoming our limitless self, and that is by unbecoming who we have believed ourselves to be: a conglomeration of projections and limitations given to us since birth. We subconsciously block our own evolution by believing we must maintain the identity we have been given or have chosen. We are so much more than we can begin to believe we are, but begin to believe we must. Believe in ourselves. Trust ourselves. Trust in ourselves. How could we possibly give ourselves a better gift than that of self-love and respect through acceptance of our own Divinity? Always and in all ways trust and believe in yourself.

## Your Relationship With Yourself

When we believe in something, we give it energy. This gives it life and meaning. The same applies in reverse. If we don't believe in something we don't give it energy, and it does not exist within our journey. With this knowledge, it makes more sense to believe in yourself, than not believing in yourself. Bringing you back to life, with trust, will propel your evolution and truly change your life in many ways. Breathe new life into you. Look for your beauty instead of punishing yourself. The rewards of trusting and believing in yourself will outweigh any and all negative thoughts you may have about yourself. All it takes is to implement a new mindset, which will eventually replace many old patterns and beliefs about how you see yourself. Look for the good within, not dwelling on the things you don't like about you. This ensures a successful inner environment, leading to a happiness you've been looking for. Give yourself this awareness, and your life will change exponentially for the better. Your relationship with yourself is the most important one you'll ever have. Give it the chance you deserve.

## Respecting Our Healing Journey

Our journey of emotional healing is so well embedded in the Divine timing of our Spirit, guides, and angels that what we are meant to heal at a given time will present itself naturally and rise without force. I have come, through my own deep healing journey, into having the deepest respect for my own dissociative survival mechanisms.

This, we cannot approach with our masculine energy and force things to light before their time, as we would only re-traumatize ourselves. Here, we need the supportive embrace, love, acceptance, and patience of our own feminine energy, to be held and nurtured back to life. Our masculine energy, however, is needed to create new healthy boundaries, to remain grounded in reality, and to help us come back out of victim mode. This journey is so intricate, as we are dealing with deep, soul crushing developmental traumas, that its direction and timing truly belong in the hands of our higher guidance.

The support from a trustworthy person, however, is invaluable in being able to voice our pains, reintegrate our emotions, and have someone hold a safe, loving space for us, while we fall apart and face our deepest pains. As we are doing this inner work, we are slowly, gently excavating the precious being that got buried underneath heaps of pain, patriarchal conditioning, violent projections, and shaming. Bit by bit, we are coming alive again and reclaiming our authenticity and personal freedom.

We are getting to know ourselves for the first time, and re-learning the simple things that we forgot, like trusting and believing in ourselves, and truly being good to ourselves. There is nothing more sacred than allowing ourselves to evolve and become who we are meant to be.

## Coming Out Of Survival Mode

Finding the courage to truly face ourselves is a prerequisite for our personal freedom. The journey of coming out of survival mode and hiding requires that we go deep within ourselves and find acceptance, willingness, trust, love, compassion, and a fierce determination to no longer be stuck in the smallness of our comfort zone. The fruits of all the emotional healing work we have done are waiting to be harvested. But we have to open the cocoon we have been hiding in, come out, and fully embrace the life that is ours to live. Take a deep breath and be proud of who you are becoming and how far you have come. Trust and do not be afraid of being free.

# How To Make It Through Volatile Times

There is much unrest within our outer world during these times that is continually bombarding us with negativity. So, how can we navigate our way through any volatile period of time? To begin with, we must not lose hope and faith. We are on the cusp of many wonderful things, so please remember everything has purpose and happens as it is meant to. Now is the time for way showers and light bringers to dig deep within, and spread your light to be a beacon for those in need. We're not here to save anyone, but we all must band together and support each other. Look at the big picture, and know that everything that's happening is bringing awareness to what needs to be healed as a civilization, and it will be healed. There must be chaos before there is order. Don't allow yourself to take on the energies of the outer world. Focus on your own Divinity, your inner light, and don't allow yourself to be brought down by being in survival or victim mode. Within you is all you need, so go within, not the outer world, to find your own inner peace. Live every aspect of your life from the heart, and remember that God doesn't abandon us, we forget. Don't lose hope for we have been promised a New Day, and a New Way. Focus on this promise, and remember to trust. We don't need to know why it's happening; we simply need to trust.

# You Owe No Loyalty To Your Ancestor's Limitations

Allow yourself to step outside of the box that you were born into. Let the tight conditioning, the smallness, the grey obedience go. Breathe and take up space. Splash some color around. There is a wildness in your cells, a blueprint for your life in accordance with your Divine Spirit that will unfold if you permit it. There is a song within your bones that wants to find expression. Don't be afraid of being fully you. Yes, it takes courage after everything you have been through. But who really cares how you live your life. It is yours to live, anyway. You owe no loyalty to your ancestor's limitations. Learn to boldly trust yourself and your inner guidance. Give yourself permission to experiment, make mistakes, learn, and grow. Life doesn't need to be neatly controlled, as we were taught by anxious perfectionists. Being on this planet is by nature messy. We don't know where we are going or what the next moment will bring. Truly, all we have is our trust in ourselves and the Divine, unbecoming everything along the way that does not agree with our true authenticity. This alone will elevate us on our journey and bring us home to ourselves.

## Going Into Our Darkness

Sometimes life becomes dark and difficult. We have trouble finding hope and beauty, and it seems that we have fallen out of who we normally are, and into some deep hole inside. Who we were a moment ago, our strength, control, and confidence, have vanished and we don't know how to get ourselves back to our comfort zone. In this place, we may not like to socialize or be out in the open. We just want to be in our cave and figure out what's wrong with us.

The objective, however, of being in this internal place of pain may not be to pull ourselves back out and go back to who we were. This may not be a space to escape from in a hurry, but to allow and surrender into. The Universe may have conspired to bring us here, so that we can face something about ourselves that we haven't been able to before, allowing a new layer of healing that is being presented to us.

It takes enormous trust to be able to go deep inside ourselves, into the darkness that we cannot tolerate. But when we find ourselves among our seeping wounds, immersed in the pain we have previously avoided, we suddenly have no choice but to slow down and allow what is happening. We encounter a side of ourselves that we don't get to know in our daily lives of surface dwelling. Here, all we can do is invite the misfit consciousnesses inside to gather round and comfort each other. When we accept all that exists on the deeper levels of our psyche, we actually find a new intimacy with ourselves, a new strength, a calmer presence. Sitting in the midst of our own devastation, with nowhere to run or hide, we learn that we are much better off just accepting our predicament with patience and compassion. We can then allow this opportunity to heal, learn, and grow from being so deep inside ourselves.

Every time we go to this internal place where we have no control, we embrace our vulnerability a bit more. This fertile darkness is where our evolution happens and where a new version of ourselves is being born out of the ashes of the old. Yet, we must not prematurely lift ourselves back into the light we are accustomed to, but allow the natural process of what is happening with as much trust as we can muster.

Our journey of unbecoming is not under our control, but firmly in the loving hands of our Spirit and guides. And we must learn to trust them implicitly, so that we can know without a doubt that they will never abandon us and leave us here in the dark. There is purpose to this, and they will make sure that it is being fulfilled. They guard and guide our metamorphosis, our journey of evolution, with our highest good always at heart.

## Gratitude For Who We Were In The Past

We all have been many different people in this lifetime. This is evolution, as we are no longer who we were. Those periods in our life, the multitude of hats we wore, the personalities we were… need to receive gratitude from us now. Thank them for bringing forth who you are today, for without them, life would not be as it is. Thank those past mistakes, for you learned from them. Thank those broken hearts, for they taught us how to love on a deeper level. Thank those bad decisions with forgiveness because we grew knowledge and wisdom from them. Give gratitude for those who taught us how to be, and how not to be. Forgive your former selves for not knowing better, for they taught you that difference. They deserve to see us be the best version of ourselves that we can be for today, as they are our biggest fan who only wants the best for us. Wear your battle scars with pride, let that person go, knowing they will always be a huge part of you. Hold them tight to your heart as you help them heal their pains and traumas, for you, together, are building the current and future you.

# Teach The Children Well

A child knows nothing, other than what they are taught. As a parent, grandparent, aunt, uncle, family friend, or neighbor... what are you teaching them? They see our behavioral patterns, all of them, and believe they are always acceptable, not knowing any different. Our angry outbursts, boundaries, or lack thereof, our laughter, tears, fists, love, our words of projection onto others, the list is never ending. Adults are their first role models, and they are sponges, ready to be the apple of our eyes, looking for acceptance. They mimic our every move, our attitudes, our every nuance, because we are their only measure of what is acceptable. So, what are you teaching the children in your life? Teach them love, respect, honor, dignity - all the things we've learned in life that really mean something. Be their example of what is right and just. Give them a foundation to succeed. What we teach them is also our contribution toward building a better future.

## Connecting With Mother/Father God

There is order in the higher realms. Nothing is random. All Lightbeings have a special place, and special role. It is, in its own right, an etheric society that is living, learning, and evolving with each other, though each Spirit has its own journey within the Oneness. There are many dimensions and realms. Most of us who feel a connection with the Divine have tiny glimpses - that is all. The bigger picture eludes us completely. We have been given the nuisance of amnesia at birth, and cannot remember who we are and where we came from. As we are awakening and opening our hearts, our glimpses may get stronger, our yearning for our real home in the etheric may get louder. As we draw closer to the center of our hearts, the seat of our Spirit, we may have openings of our psychic abilities. These are completely natural and inherent in everyone. So, if you feel that you are hearing the voice of God, please remember that the messenger is never what is important. It is the message that is of essence. Too many people have claimed, throughout the centuries, to have special favor with God, to be extra loved. And too many folks, who came here to this planet to be of service during this shift, are navel gazing, believing that they, themselves, have become a deity. To know Mother/Father God, to whatever tiny degree, is to be naturally humble. Not in self-punishment, or lowering ourselves, but in unending gratitude and by knowing our place, also to whatever degree, in the greater scheme of things, and not assuming a position that is not ours to take on. Simply by living with a heart filled with love and fulfilling our soul contracts, are we honoring the Divine. Trust deeply and find what your personal connection to the Divine Consciousness feels like. For me, there is a warm feeling of being safe and being loved and cared for, personally and specifically, more deeply than any human conception. I feel known and accepted by my true, eternal Divine Parents, who are always, always there for me.

## Happy At Heart

Happiness is only possible in the state of connectedness. This is why the kind people, the empathic people who include that which exists around them, are the happiest at heart. They are literally at peace with themselves because they know they are embedded in a larger web of life, even if it is not consciously known. When we give to another, we are reaching beyond the limits of the 3D, and in that moment, we are touching something larger than ourselves. This is why there is a sense of elation when we are giving from the heart with discernment and healthy boundaries. It is nurturing. It feeds us, as well. It is where we expand and shine our light. We are, in that moment, the embodiment of love in action. What higher purpose could there be?

## Overcoming Near Impossible Odds

Drive, determination, and dedication are essential to completing any task or endeavor we can possibly undertake. Drive is derived by a basic need or desire to begin. Determination is the mindset necessary for endurance to see them come to fruition. Dedication is the belief and trust of the self within, to make sure every detail is understood and accepted. With these in mind, we assure ourselves success. I learned these three rules during recovery from a major stroke thirty years ago. I found that I had the strength and courage to overcome the paralysis and inability to speak, and was back to work in nine months, despite being told I wouldn't survive. I was told that someone would have to care for me the rest of my life, as I would never walk or talk again. We all have this within us. It's your task to go within and find that all you need is readily available and accessible. The only thing many lack is trusting and believing in ourselves enough to make an effort. The first step is the mindset. You have the ability to do just about anything once you have made up your mind that it is going to happen. Trust and believe in yourself always and in all ways, and make it happen.

# Finding Beauty In The Darkness

As we personally come out of the trauma of a natural disaster, our external landscape has been forever changed. It will eventually become a beautiful sight to behold, as nature adapts to its new normal. For those of us affected by the trauma, our internal landscape was also forever changed. We had to accept the experiences and learn to move on from the devastation. It doesn't need to be a crisis for us to accept a new normal, which could be even more beautiful for our inward journey. Each and every pain and trauma we endure changes us on many planes and levels. If we choose to adapt to the changes within, we find that this is how we evolve. We become stronger, more confident within ourselves, and now we have a new reference point from which to grow. Even within the destruction of our lands, many of us saw the beauty that came from that experience. There is always beauty within any darkness when we can see beyond our pains. I truly believe change is the only constant in our lives, so we need to be able to accept the changes, making it easier for us to adapt. Within the perception of staying in victim mentality, we are unable to see beauty, therefore, unable to move beyond our pains and traumas. You have the opportunity to roll with the changes to learn, heal, and grow from any experience. Change your perception, change your life. Embrace and adapt to the changes without resistance and allow your evolution. Inspire yourself to rise above what was. There is always beauty to be found, especially within the self.

## The Inward Journey Of Awakening

When we have awareness, recognition, and acceptance of our awakening journey, there is no longer a need to keep looking for anything on our journey. We surrender and allow life to come to us as it is meant to be. There is no longer a need to believe there is anything to manifest or attract because it is already present within us, and at this point our efforts become our blocks, hindering an organic process. All we need to do is go within, heal what is coming to the forefront, accept our own Divinity, and live every aspect of our lives from the heart, realizing our true essence is a state of love. This all can be achieved through trusting and believing in ourselves, and living in the moment, with the understanding that everything outside of this moment is an illusion. We need to trust the process, and that the Universe will bring exactly what we need for our journey and evolution. We let go of the illusion that we can control our lives, and the experiences life brings us, and give ourselves permission to experience without judgment. Our awakening journey is within, not without. There is no need to keep looking for something we already possess. Without trust there can be no evolution, and without trust we will never be able to realize our true authentic self… our Spirit.

# Getting To Know Your Self

I honestly don't believe we must be able to identify what we are feeling emotionally, nor do we have to understand it. We simply honor it and give space to exist within. It doesn't mean we allow it to run our lives, and we certainly don't have to become it. Perhaps it belongs to the Collective Consciousness, or it's from a past life. One rule I live by, in balance, is to allow the Higher self to take care of the etheric, while the 3D runs the mundane of the body and mind. This allows us to focus on what we need, catering to both in balance. It's honestly one of the hardest lessons I have been learning on my awakening and healing journey. There has to be an incredible amount of awareness of the self, on the deepest levels possible for today. Tomorrow, we go a little deeper, until we no longer exist on this plane. This is just one of our purposes: to evolve. This process is never ending, and I believe it will last lifetimes in the future. With every new incarnation, we are given new opportunities to learn, heal, and grow, but it doesn't mean we have to know all the why's and wherefores. Know your own energy signature and I assure you that life will become way smoother. Get to know you… personally.

## The Importance of Trusting Our Guides

Our life journey has already been laid out by our Spirit, as it was contracted before we incarnated. While we have been gifted free will, which we can apply at any moment to any part of our life, we are wise to follow the guidance of our inner Divinity. Our 3D self and the wounded consciousnesses within habitually assert themselves and take control of our life. This will lead to a life of turmoil and suffering because the decisions that our bodily self makes differ greatly from that of our Spirit. Above all, our cellular self seeks comfort, safety, and familiarity. We like status quo and knowing exactly what to expect.

Our Spirit, however, has a very different perspective. It is highly concerned with our mental, emotional, physical wellbeing, and highest good. It is often up against the resistance of the 3D self in its attempts to guide us to where we need to be from a higher perspective. Our 3D self may have hopes, dreams, goals, and expectations that we want fulfilled exactly in the way that we envision them. As human beings we are solutionists. We like having the answers and being in the know. We cannot stand not knowing, not having the answers, not understanding, or not having a previous reference for what is going on. And if we do not know, rather than embracing the unknown, we fill in the blank and make up a story that suits our needs.

But where, in this morbid existence of predictable grayness and stagnant energy are you really alive? Where are you free to be yourself, to express your authenticity? Where is your courage, your will, your love, and passion? How long have you perpetuated the patterns that have kept you three quarter numb and cut off from your essence? Is just living in the 3D really enough? Are you not much larger than that? Is not the spark in your eyes a part of the Divine eternal self that animates your body? Are you not a part of God, woven out of the same fabric? And is it not excruciatingly painful and boring to make yourself so small?

We have all been conditioned - generation after generation - to keep ourselves quiet and small, after enduring all kinds of atrocities at the hands of strangers and those we trusted the most. Having lived in survival mode for so long, we don't remember how it feels to truly be alive, and to embrace the moment with the excitement of a child. To deeply breathe, and be relaxed and at ease within our bodies. We have forgotten so much, including what life is really about.

Deep down, we feel so separate, so lonely, so small, and unworthy, our perspective often narrowed to just ourselves. Yet, we insist that we are capable of guiding ourselves on a moment-to-moment basis to a better life. Our journey of self-guidance started when the traumas occurred early in our life, and when we were cut off from our awareness of our own Spirit. We slammed shut so hard when we were abused that we lost awareness of who we are.

No longer being guided by the Spirit - in our awareness, though not in truth - we assumed the leadership role that we thought was vacant. From then on, we stumbled more or less blindly through our lives. Yet, behind the scenes we were still ever so lovingly guided by our Divine Spirit, and our guides and angels. They tried to align us with our highest good and with the contracts that we signed and promised to fulfill. Tirelessly, our guides have been by our side every moment of our days and nights, trying to instill in us a sense of trusting ourselves and trusting them.

I cannot imagine the patience that is needed for Them to watch us ignore their guidance, and wander aimlessly about in a self-guided frenzy that has us feeling busy and maybe important, yet often without accomplishments that would mean anything to our Spirit.

Many of us have experienced and witnessed that the more we are in alignment with our Spirit, allowing ourselves to be guided by its wisdom and knowledge, the smoother our earthly lives will become. This does not mean that there are not ups and downs, but with the connection to our Spirit open, we are so much better equipped to handle the challenges that come our way. We listen and do as we have been told or shown by our higher guidance, who knows and sees so far beyond what we can possibly imagine.

The more we become aware of our guides, the more we are able to recognize them as our companions in the etheric, many of whom have been with us since we were born. Some of them are ancestors from our earthly lineage, some are our home-planet family, and dearest soul mates. Among them are mentors from past lives, and members from our eternal soul group with whom we have incarnated time and again, on different planets including this one. Some are from the angelic realms. Our guides are definitely no strangers to us. Their love for us is ancient.

Given their combined wisdom, and their knowledge of us and the specifics of our ways, are they not in an excellent position to guide us, always and in every moment, into the heart of our true north? Then trust well, my friends, and practice that which you yet lack, so that one day your heart will be so filled with trust that you will have lost interest in guiding yourself from a limited perspective.

You will have complete willingness to be exactly where you are meant to be and to experience life on life's terms, not your own. Trust will permeate every fiber of your being, and you will know a deep inner peace, feeling absolutely safe and loved. And your cup of gratitude will be filled with utter wonder at all the gifts that life bestows upon you, despite the myriads of challenges and hardships you may face. You will know, without a doubt, that you are carried and protected by this marvelous ethic collaboration of loved ones in the higher dimensions.

## We Are Not Failing

Many of us try incredibly hard to live a life worthy of our journey. At times, it seems as if our efforts are an exercise in futility. It appears as if we just can't seem to get it right, and it doesn't seem that we are moving forward and in the right direction. Two ideas come to mind during these crises. Not everything is as it seems. Our perception becomes skewed by our frustration at not receiving our applied intentions. But most importantly, life is one huge experiment. We never fail until we give up and admit defeat, but in retrospect, we can clearly see a way that didn't work, and we keep trying. My point, my friends, is we must be diligent in our efforts to trust. We keep trying regardless of our thought that we are failing. No inventor, scientist, or anyone who has become successful caved into a self-defeating pattern of giving up. Ask the Divine to show you what you need to see and hear. Look for subliminal and gentle messages, ones we may be overlooking. Often the answers we seek are simplistic and right before our eyes. Allow it to present itself. Don't look for just what you want to hear or see. That's just trying to control the Universe, which is an absolute exercise in futility.

# Willingness To Change

Changing a mindset is one way of stepping outside of our perception to see a truth we have been unable to properly see. Ask yourself this simple question: Can I be successful within the current mindset I have existed within? If you are truly honest with yourself, the answer will always be no. There is always a need to expand where we are coming from and how we perceive. This is how we evolve. Change is inevitable, and resistance to change will only bring us needless suffering and hardship. Openness and willingness to allow change will facilitate the process of bringing a higher understanding of who we are. This is in part self-mastery and part of our awakening journey. Allow and accept what is meant to be and simplify any aspect of your life. Find the courage and strength that you have within, and step outside of your comfort zone. Embrace your vulnerability. This is how we learn, heal, and grow.

## Living In the Present

"Forever is our today...," written by Brian May of Queen. So many of us are fixated on the future while we reside in the past. Neither exist. We only have the current moments that create the present. We dream passionately of a better future for ourselves, but if we can't be present in the now, then it will be elusive. It's always good to look to the future, but life happens in the here and now, not the future. We place all of our hopes and dreams on what we believe will be a better day. Take that energy used on tomorrow and build your future today. Taking an active role in our lives means we do today as we can, to build the foundation necessary to succeed. The past holds all we need to heal in order to strengthen the building blocks of our entire existence. The way to the future is stepping out of the past and into this moment. Our pains and traumas of the past have become blocks in our evolution. If you truly want to realize a better day, a better way, then this moment is the right time to make it happen. Focus your energy inward, with your passion of living a better tomorrow, and I guarantee you will make great headway toward your goals. If we don't place importance on giving reality to our intentions, then they mean nothing. Take steps to ensure your actions are making a change today for a brighter tomorrow.

# Gratitude At the End of the Day

Every night I give gratitude to Mother, Father, God, my guides, ancestors, and my Light teams. I do this, because no matter how crappy my day was, I was gifted a day to experience and evolve. I was given another day to learn, heal, and grow. For all of this, I am incredibly grateful. I don't care if my day was not so kind, or I had an amazingly great day. I'm giving gratitude. It brings me past any desire to feel sorry for myself, or even remain in victim mentality. I am able to see beauty, where earlier, I felt anger. I took time to allow my emotional self to process the events of the day, becoming the observer to see beyond my current perception. Indeed, my 3D self needs to process events from the eyes of the Spirit self to see truth. It is necessary for our evolution to honor what we feel, without becoming it or projecting our emotions onto others. It's all about the mindset of allowing what is meant to be. It's about allowing a day to be what it is, without our judgment. We choose to see our experience either through the eyes of the Spirit or the eyes of the ego. Knowing to choose the Spirit will indeed propel us farther than choosing our woundedness.

# Surrendering Our Need For Control

Usually, we surrender only in extreme situations, but if we are to evolve and awaken, we have to learn to let go of our compulsive need to control everything. We must learn to trust ourselves and God again, relax and allow life to come to us. Every day provides us with opportunity to choose trust and surrender over fear and control, and to break the generational patterns and beliefs that were projected onto us. Control creates suffering for all parts of the self, including the body. It becomes acidic and prone to illness. The constant state of anxiety and contraction creates toxins that foster chemical imbalances within the body. The compulsion for control is an empty habitual survival mechanism, an illusion that serves no purpose, as it does not actually keep us safe. It blocks our authenticity and freedom, and keeps us bound to continually living in fear. While we are operating from control, we can neither truly give, nor can we receive because we are blocking the flow of life through us and to us. When we surrender and live in a state of trust, everything softens and the body can regain its health, the mind can find balance, the heart feel joy, and the Spirit express its true Divine nature. Every day we surrender as much as we can, and layer by layer we are building a new foundation for our personal freedom.

# Personal Boundaries

We aren't always the driving force that brings unwanted drama and heartache into our lives. All too often we are brought into other people's pain and trauma, whether we want to or not. It doesn't mean we have to accept the energy of their projections. Allow them to vent, just the same as you sometimes need to vent, but don't allow them to project. Setting healthy personal boundaries shows others how we need to be treated, with the respect we deserve. If they feel the need to blow past your limitations, then perhaps we should question our relationship with them. Be forgiving with the occasional, and stern with their patterns. Ask them from your heart to please adhere to your boundaries, and if they won't, then perhaps it's best to walk away from the situation. We can no longer allow others to treat us however they wish. This is self-love and self-respect. We are setting our personal boundaries and living by them.

## Nurturing Our Body Back To Health

Most of us have abused our own body in the same way that we were raised and treated by others. Like the generations before us, we had no positive relationship with our precious fleshy vessel, and pushed it, year after year, past the point of exhaustion without giving back to it. We ignored its needs and communications, and expected our body to just keep on functioning and performing, without paying attention to the stressors we allowed into our lives.

Most of us unconsciously projected a lot of self-hatred and shaming onto our cellular self. Now, many of us are forced through some form of health crisis to change our relationship with our physicality, and stop all forms of self-abuse. We are learning to pay attention to our body's actual needs for fresh air, movement, rest, customized nutrition, and self-care. While we previously may have allowed our inner child or wounded ego to determine our food intake according to their standards of maximizing comfort or eating away our sorrows, we are now forced to make internal changes, and take control of our health.

We are learning that there is a difference between consuming what we grew up with, and what is cheap and convenient, versus actually nurturing our body with what it requires at a bio-chemical level, via the proper nutrition that keeps us in good health. Paying attention and listening inward in a new way, we are able to discern what we need to intake to keep our bio-chemical machine working properly, and not just filling our stomach with more illness causing toxins. As we are building a new relationship with ourselves at all levels, we are up against our need for creature comfort and the familiar. Yet, if we stay on the same track that we have been on for so long, we will eventually destroy our vessel.

It takes courage and enormous willpower to implement any changes, from quitting an addiction to changing our food habits of comfort and convenience. But once we make the changes, start feeling better, and have more energy, we cannot even imagine going back to how sluggish, heavy, clouded, and unwell we felt before taking charge of our life, and truly nurturing soul and soma with an ever-increasing awareness of self-love.

# The Rewarding Journey of Deep Healing

When we cannot trust and allow, we are living within the limitations of what is familiar from the past, controlling every aspect of our lives from the perspective of a fear-based mind. No evolution is possible when we exist merely in our heads, knowing the spiritual concepts, but not living from the heart. This is the state of the unhealed. To change this, we will have to embrace all that we are, including our wounded ego, traumatized inner child, and Divine, loving Spirit. We have to open up the caverns of repressed emotions, and do the vulnerable inner work. The awakening process has us moving out of our comfort-zone, getting to know ourselves at the deepest levels, finding our will and our wholeness, and all the answers we are seeking within. It is a life-long emotional healing process to change the patterns and beliefs that were projected onto us. One day at a time, with compassion and courage, we excavate the precious self that we are, and learn to love and accept ourselves so deeply that outside approval is no longer necessary. Accepting help from the Divine, and doing our work, we become free to explore our uniqueness and authenticity without self-judgment, and see life through the innocent eyes of our Spirit self.

# The Demand For Abundance

Desperately wanting something on our journey can and will be the block as to why it doesn't come to us. It is about Divine timing, not ours. Remembering we have already, at the soul level, contracted for our abundance, we can let go of the attachment of our desire, and choose to stop trying to control the Universe. That just never works out for us. If I may offer a different perspective. When we don't receive what we believe we are lacking, it can have several meanings. It can be that there is something much better coming for us, this isn't the right timing, or perhaps we didn't contract for this. Having an attachment means we either have ownership, or we are being owned by the attachment. When we expect to be given anything, we have a predetermined outcome, an expectation. That in itself is incredibly controlling, and we have become entitled to the demand of our desire. Truthfully, we are entitled to what we have contracted for, and we never have had the ability to control what comes to us. With as much grace as possible, let go of the demand and take the importance we believe we need off of the issue. In other words, step out of the lack mentality and allow what is divinely inherent to come to us with ease in every aspect of our lives. Just because the Divine is within us, doesn't mean we are a god.

## The Vulnerability of Evolution

I pray you all come to a point on your journey, where you are so far removed from your former self that you no longer know who you are. You'll find there are no longer viable reference points from which to draw. Your cellular will carry all the memories, emotions, pains, and traumas of your former self, but they will feel distant, almost like someone else's. You no longer know who you are, but at the same time you are very much the same being. It simply means that you have come to a juncture on your path where you have everywhere to go. Freedom! All you need to do, is allow your Spirit to carry you to the next phase of evolution. We reinvent who we are every day, to become our authentic self. Now, you've reached this point of becoming your authentic self and knowing yourself on the deepest level you possibly can, to a point of self-mastery, and suddenly that knowing is gone. This is total vulnerability, beyond what we could imagine, as there is no longer memory of what our comfort zone even was. We become so far removed from our former self that it all seems surreal. This is your evolution.

## Live and Let Live

Spirituality is not a competition where one is either more spiritual, or less spiritual than another. That belief comes from the woundedness of the ego. The simple truth is, we're all at different places on our respective journeys. Since our journey is unique to us alone, there can be absolutely no comparison between individuals and their journeys. Not only do we have unique experiences, we interpret those experiences differently. We may have similar experiences, and we may share experiences, but we will have our own truth of it. We must remember that we all contracted for every experience brought to us, as well as the abundance in our lives. Allow them their journey and know it has absolutely nothing to do with you, so it can't be about you. Focus on keeping with your path in life, and don't worry that you don't have what they do. Besides, the grass is always greener on the other side of the fence, right? Not always, especially since we have no clue what they contracted for. This is why our focus is on us and no one else. Live and let live.

## Practicing Discernment During These Times

The cosmic energies currently streaming onto our planet are forcing out people's authenticity and who they are beneath the surface. Those of us on a conscious journey of light are growing and evolving in leaps and bounds toward a heart-centered existence in alignment with our own Spirit. The people in denial, living unaware over top of their suppressed emotions, however, are going one of two directions: they are either fading away into depression and more self-defeating patterns, or they are acting out in aggression and violence toward others. People are losing it fast. Under these energies, mental illnesses are progressing at an unprecedented rate. Practice utmost discernment and listen to your intuition. Don't ignore the signs and guidance given to you by your Spirit and guides. Trust yourself more than ever. Even those close to us may show increased toxic behavior. Keep your eyes wide open and walk away from crazy. Don't enable those who shy away from accountability. Stay focused on your journey and don't let yourself be drawn into someone else's conflict. It's not worth it and you have a bright mission to fulfill at this time.

# Advice From My Spirit To My Younger Selves

There is one particular piece of advice I would like to give my younger selves and their many aspects. Value your freedom. Next to your belief in yourself and the Divine, this will mean much more as you get older. The hard work you've done to become who you are is amazing. I know what you've experienced, and I know the depths of your darkness you have traversed. I'm so very proud of you and your accomplishments. You've healed lifetimes of anguish and altered the course of your ancestral path. You've shared your healing with the Collective, and allowed others to learn, heal, and grow form your own reconciliations. You found your light in the depths of your own pains and traumas, and overcame insurmountable odds. You've corrected many past mistakes and learned to live from the heart. As your Spirit self, I can say with honor how proud I am of you. Because of your diligence and determination, you've stayed true to your journey. You've found how to love yourself, and allowed yourself to receive love. Thank you for what you have endured, for without you, we would not be us today. With all the loving gratitude and grace I possess, I honor you for becoming who you are today. Thank you.

## Embracing Our Darkness

Sometimes life becomes dark and difficult. We have trouble finding hope and beauty, and it seems that we have fallen out of who we normally are, and into some deep hole inside. Who we were a moment ago, our strength, control, and confidence, have vanished and we don't know how to get ourselves back to our comfort zone. In this new place, we don't like to socialize or be out in the open. We just want to be in our cave and figure out what's wrong with us.

The objective, however, of being in this internal place of pain may not be to pull ourselves back out and go back to who we were. This may not be a space to escape from in a hurry, but to allow and surrender into. The Universe may have conspired to bring us here, so we can face something about ourselves that we haven't been able to before, allowing a new layer of healing.

It takes enormous trust to be able to go deep inside ourselves into the darkness that we can barely tolerate. But when we find ourselves among our seeping wounds, and faced with an abyss of pain, we suddenly have no choice but to slow down and allow what is happening. We encounter a side of ourselves that we don't know in our daily lives of surface dwelling. Here, all we can do is invite the misfit consciousnesses inside to gather round and comfort each other. When we accept all that exists on the deeper levels of our psyche with love, we actually find a new intimacy with ourselves, a new strength, and calmer presence.

Sitting in the midst of our own devastation, with nowhere to run or hide, we learn that we are much better off just accepting our predicament with compassion, and looking to where we can learn, heal, and grow from being so deep inside ourselves. Every time we go to this internal place where we have no control we embrace our vulnerability a bit more. This fertile darkness is where our evolution happens, and where a new version of ourselves is being born out of the ashes of the old. Yet, we must not prematurely lift ourselves back into the light we are accustomed to, but allow the natural process of what is happening with as much trust as we can muster.

Our journey of unbecoming is not under our control, but firmly in the loving hands of our Spirit and guides. And we must learn to trust them implicitly so that we can know without a doubt that they would never abandon us and leave us here in the dark. There is purpose to this, and they will make sure that it is being fulfilled. They guard and guide our metamorphosis, our journey of evolution, with our highest good always at heart.

## Living In Our Natural State

None of us can begin to understand, let alone know, the will of God. What we can do, absolutely, is have trust that we will be provided for, even in the darkest of times. I can't express the need for trust enough, especially as we navigate this unknown called life and what it's going to bring us. How do we trust so deeply to accept that we are, indeed, living as we are meant to? Simply, by living in a state of love, living from the heart-centered self, and allowing our Spirit to guide us. This is as we are meant to be, in our natural state, love. In this state, there cannot be hatred for others. We can't possibly be in this natural state and look down upon others to make ourselves bigger. There is no hierarchy in spirituality since we all come from the same Source. I have stated before of my belief that we are like apples from a tree, each unique from others but also a part of each other. Now, more than ever, we need to band together and help one another through this shared journey of the Collective Consciousness. Now is the time to heal old patterns and beliefs, and become our authentic selves. We strengthen as a whole and weaken as one. Go within and become that which you came here to be. Always listen with your heart and you'll evolve organically.

# How Our Guides Help Us with Our Healing

Some of us have suffered so deeply in this life. And our hearts are still filled with much pain and despair. We may try to find beauty in life, but it is hard for us to breathe and take life in, let alone be with ourselves. If this is your reality, please know that you are deeply loved and held. Your ancestors, guides, and angels comfort you every day and care deeply about you. They work hard to bring you little glimmers of hope and happiness, even if they are fleeting.

If you can find the courage within to face your pain, you will start unravelling the knot and create movement. This doesn't mean that your pain and traumas will miraculously be gone, but you will make progress. And in time you will find that life takes on a whole new quality. You will no longer be stuck in an internal prison, but ride the waves of life's ups and downs with an attitude of allowance. There will be times when you are deeply healing and processing what happened to you, shedding tears that you never could before. And there will be times when you have purged much, and feel like you just came out of the laundry, fresh and clean with brightness.

If you can allow this joint venture - with your guides and Spirit - of healing your past so that your future can be different, you will have much inner work to do. But every time you permit another aspect of your past to come to the surface and be healed, and work with it as best you can, you have created much movement. Then your guides can come in and remove what is no longer needed.

As such, your process of letting go is quantum. You get it loosened, feel your emotions, and process deeply, with a willingness to let go and not hold on, and painful memories and energetic chords get transmuted by your etheric helpers, so that you can move onto the next layer. It is truly teamwork to heal in such a manner, and a grand metamorphosis that spans several dimensions. If you really want to heal and receive the continuous help of your guides, just ask them to show you and help you with awareness. Communicate with them even if you are not sure if you are hearing them. They hear you and respond.

Over time, it will be more natural to be involved in this collaborative dance of healing. Your gratitude will be immense for those walking this life with you, every second of each day and night, caring for you and your healing so deeply. Becoming aware of this process, alone, will bring a light back into your heart, as you find gratitude for your ancestors and mighty companions on your earthly journey. They not only make your healing faster, but possible.

# Keeping Up With Our Internal Changes

The reference points from yesterday are outdated for today's experience. We can no longer rely on yesterday's truth as our truth today. Because we are in a state of constant change, nothing we have experienced will prepare us for what we are currently going through, no matter how similar the situations. It may offer us a guideline, but the nuances and particulars don't match with today's experience. Since we are no longer the same being today as we were yesterday, we must look at it from the perspective of our current self. The person we were yesterday no longer exists. Seeing from a perspective that is no more, will only keep us in that time. Until we move on from every yesterday, we shall remain there, unable to move forward. There is no normalcy in life as we knew it because we all are being guided to live in this moment, which is all we have. The here and now dictate our lives, not our past, especially in how we respond or react. If we keep looking back, expecting to see ourselves, we aren't going to notice who we are today. That person has evolved beyond what was. Keeping up with our internal changes is challenging at best, but necessary to master the self and who we are transforming into. Embrace this moment and allow the changes of evolution to come.

# Overcoming Our Need To Control Everything

There comes a point on our journey where we are faced with a tough decision. As humans, we want to be in control of everything around us and within us, and many of us actually enjoy dominating our environment. We want to live in a world where everyone thinks like us, and affirms who we believe we are by being the same way.

Since we were born, we have been molded by every institution through control of our thoughts, emotions, and behaviors, and we have adopted these habits and patterns of fear. To spend even an hour without controlling something and arranging it to our liking is near impossible for us.

The spiritual trend of manifesting often is an expression of our compulsive need to have everything just the way we want it, instead of trusting. The decision we have to make is between our own freedom and furthering of our evolution, and our cellular habitual need to stay in control of everything. We can't have it both ways.

We may have the concepts down, but that is not the same as actually learning to trust and unclench, and allow life to come to us as it is meant to be. This heavy internal conflict is what most of us are up against, and no one is above this. If we want to evolve and reconnect with our Divinity, we have to do the emotional healing work.

We have to learn to rewire our brains, change our cellular blueprint, and open our hearts wide. This raw, messy undoing and unbecoming of our conditioning is at the core of our awakening process. We must do the difficult inner work to evolve.

## The Medicine of Trust

Trust is medicine. It allows us to come out of the outdated cellular patterns of codependence, conditioning, and survival, and find our freedom. It helps us let go of our need for control and transforms our fears into allowance, willingness, and acceptance. Trust is one of the cornerstones of the new foundation that we are building on our journey of self-mastery. Learning to trust ourselves will completely transform our inner world, while learning to trust the Divine again will bring us out of our devastating aloneness, and back into the universal flow of grace and love. Trust is the key to life, and without it we are hopelessly lost in our separation from source and self. Trust yourself and breathe.

## Lowering Our Walls

All of us have walls built to protect us for various and obvious reasons. For many of us, they are there so no one can get in, for some, to keep us within our comfort, or risk some type of harm. What we don't realize is that we're hiding, and many of us are hiding a gift this world really needs. We hide ourselves, not realizing we're a blessing to others. We bring to others what we are lacking, something we all need. Love. But we protect that which we value the most, our heart. We lock it up for fear of being hurt yet again. If you can't reduce your walls, then please install windows so we can see you, the blessing that's hiding. Honestly, you're keeping the rest of us from you, your gifts, your love, and our ability to return what you give us. Giving and receiving are of the same cycle, in equal measure, one to the other. It's really not better to give than receive, as they are a part of the other, in balance. Learning to allow ourselves to receive is a Sovereign Right that can and will change our lives in quantitative measure. Let us in to your heart. Please. Allow us the opportunity to give of ourselves, in gratitude.

# A Different Perspective on Being Triggered

Triggered again. Why do we keep getting triggered? Quite simply because we haven't healed the root cause. The onset of the trigger will be found within our childhood. Largely, it is a long-lost memory of pain and trauma that is related to events when we had no clue how to respond or react. We didn't have the knowledge to fully deal with that situation. So, how do we find the root cause of a reoccurring trigger? We spend time looking through the database of forgotten memories until we find a similar experience. As adults, we hopefully have the knowledge and wisdom to see that triggers show us where we need to heal. It's not a pleasant time having to rehash past painful memories, but quite necessary to move forward from those memories. While we are searching for the root cause, we will find many similar experiences connected to that one event. Eventually we will stumble across the reason(s) why we are angered. Once located we can observe how this has affected our entire life. Many memories will come flowing into our field associated with that one event. Now we are able to heal a multitude of painful memories, giving them love and reconciling our past. Just a suggestion… thank the person bringing that trigger for the opportunity to heal. They've done you a great service.

# Raising Your Vibration

Do you want to raise your vibration and truly connect with the Divine? This is not done by furthering your outward focus on spiritual rituals and fads. It is done by trusting so implicitly that you need nothing and have complete acceptance of the moment. It is done by letting go of your need for control, and surrendering your life with every fiber of your being to the Divine Mother and Father. Get to know your self at the deepest levels and embrace yourself with complete acceptance, love, and forgiveness. Let go of the expectations that you have placed on yourself, and heal your wounds. A higher frequency and dimension are not reached by doing anything, but by unclenching, breathing deeply, and allowing life to carry you to where you are meant to be, not where you imagine you want to be. You have an important part to play on this Earth. That is why you are here at this time of planetary transformation. Your alignment with your Spirit is crucial to your helpfulness according to your soul contracts. Learn to trust yourself at the deepest level. That will raise your vibration beyond your wildest dreams.

# Living From The Heart

As we learn to live from the heart in every aspect of our life, we begin to see all kinds of possibilities. We begin to find our inspiration, and we cellularly start to shift from darkness to light. As the process continues, we can see more possibilities, but now we can start to see probability. It's whittling down our narrative, becoming more specific, and clear intention is easier to find. This is our evolution. These become times of great change within, and beauty is more accessible. This forward and upward movement is the catalyst to unbecoming who we never were, to becoming authentic. Seeing things in a different light drives us to new heights of awareness. Our inner space begins to let go of what no longer serves us, and our freedom is within reach. Keep allowing the heart to open to this newness, and unimaginable magic happens within and without. Freedom is ours when we allow it to be. It is one of our sovereign rights, and indeed, good for the soul. Open your heart and your life will change. Open your heart to the authentic you – your Spirit.

## There Is Always Another Way

Within any situation or experience, we have three immediate options. Can I change my situation? If so, then change must be made. If not, then we have our second option. Can I change my perspective to find peace within my situation? For this one we really need to dig deep to find the answer. If we can, then we do. If not, then our only other option is to walk away, but before we do, we must revisit the first two and exhaust all of our options. There is always another way, sometimes beyond our perspective. Breathe deep and become the observer. Now look at your options. Unless it is a life-threatening situation, there will always be another way. Don't limit yourself to listening to your woundedness. It won't lead you anywhere near where you truly need to be. Perhaps you can't change your situation now, but is it possible in the near future? Are there plans you can make to change what really needs to be? Don't be so quick to settle on a quick fix. Sometimes it takes time to think things through. You always have options. Always and in all ways, trust and believe in yourself.

## The Unhealed Spiritual Ego

Before we were born into form, our Spirit decided upon the purpose for our incarnation – what was to be learned and healed, and the goals to be accomplished. But having free will, and life experiences that shut us off from our higher communication, most have forgotten that our body is only the vehicle for our evolution and Spirit experiences. We have become so identified with our 3D body personality that the mind has taken control as our main guidance system, based on the past and the needs of the wounded ego. Many on a spiritual or awakening journey have opened up to experiencing glimpses of their Divine self, the higher dimensions, past incarnations, and psychic gifts. But when we have not done the deep emotional healing work necessary to heal the wounded ego, and move beyond our trauma and survival patterns, the universal knowledge and gifts are often merely used to enhance the unhealed 3D body-mind personality, and fulfill our need for specialness, approval, control, status, and money. Instead of letting our precious higher experiences open us up with humility and gratitude to the raw Divine power and beauty that lies within us – and that we all share – we allow arrogance, demands for special treatment, and the belief that we own the ultimate truth to bind us to an enhanced spiritual ego. We forget that it is never about the messenger, but only about the message. And that we have a part to play in a much larger orchestration of Gods plan, as per our soul contract for this lifetime.

# Divine Sovereignty

As part of our respect for others, we must allow them to go through the hardships that their soul contracted for before this incarnation. As much as we would like to protect them from hurt, and save them from heartbreak, we cannot play god. Our role is to love them through their turmoil, give support when asked, and listen to their story as it unfolds. But it is not our role to fix them, save them, or take away their difficulties in life.

We must embrace our own helplessness, and not try to make ourselves feel better at the cost of another's experience. We usually do not understand from the human perspective why someone would contract for extended painful experiences. It is rare that we are given direct insight into another's soul contracts and purposes in this life. Because we don't know, and don't have the whole picture, it is crucial that we unlearn our compulsive need to save others. If we want to be truly helpful, then we must face our own toxic, codependent behaviors that may end up being more harmful than beneficial, despite our good intentions.

Many healers have prolonged the suffering of someone who was going to die by trying to heal them, when that person had contracted for their illness as their exit from their earthly existence. We must lose the arrogance of trying to force our version of "good" onto those around us, dictating what their experiences should be. We are slowly learning that we cannot "manifest" our will over top of everything else, and bend the Universe to our desires.

Giving others our trust that they are able to handle their life lessons will empower them, while trying to save them will communicate to them that they are incapable of taking care of themselves, and that they are inferior to us. Many of us have learned the role of family hero from an early age on, and don't know how not to try and take care of others, making their burdens our responsibility. As we are unraveling our own conditioning and embracing our authenticity, we are able to trust ourselves more. We are learning healthy boundaries, the difference between pity and empathy, and what it means to hold space for another.

It is natural to want the best for those close to us, and it is easy to get caught up in desperately wanting to help. But we must find our place with honesty, boundaries, grace, and a healthy measure of humility. We are learning to give acceptance to what is, allowing others to feel their own feelings, and work their way through their difficulties. We must respect and honor another's journey to such a degree that we don't make it about us, but allow them the Divine Sovereignty to live their lives according to their nature and soul path. This encourages and empowers them to go inward and find their own answers according to their Divinity.

# The Inner Child Is Our Connection To The Divine

I don't believe we were meant to remember the trauma of coming into this world, otherwise, we'd all have that memory. I say "trauma" because the Spirit had to find a way to fit into that small body, and our Spirit self can be massive in comparison. When we arrived in this incarnation, we were fresh from the etheric and completely within the Divine energy. As we aged, we lost that connection, becoming someone other than our authentic self. God became a distant memory, lost within the jaded being into which we developed. Your inner child remembers that Divine connection, but they, too, became frozen in time from their traumas. It's time to bring them back into your life and allow them to help you regain that Divine remembrance. Many of our emotional pains and traumas began early in life. Bring your youngling back into your heart, and they will show you where you need to heal. As they heal, they will show you, the adult, how to be free again. Regain your freedom and your connection with the Divine.

# Planting Seeds Of Light For The Future

Those of us on any type of journey of the light find being "normal" just doesn't work. Indeed, we're the ones that are different. Special, as some say? Absolutely not. Unique, yes. We all come from the same apple tree, yet all unique unto ourselves, individuals connected through an etheric string. We have difficulty on the 3D plane, with its constructs and limitations. Some would agree that we don't belong here on Earth. But we do! We volunteered to come here at this crucial time of the ascension of Mother Earth, and the evolution of its inhabitants. We all came here for specific purposes with contracts to fulfill. We have the honor of rebuilding the foundation of humanity, our future children, grandchildren, and many others of our bloodlines. We have been gifted many opportunities to change the world collectively. We are beacons to those seeking something better in their lives. We don't need to speak of it all the time, but the seeds we plant will, in time, grow. Be humble in your ways. Those meant to follow us will, the others will continue their journey just like us. Dedicate to your journey and watch in wonder as the world around you does, indeed, change.

## Living Life On Life's Terms

"Don't interject yourself," a wise person told me recently. It's been working on me ever since. How do I not interject myself into every moment, every situation, every thought, every emotion? I interject myself into everything, and have an opinion about all things. It is through my own perception that I see the world. And I am eager to expand it by knowing what's going on and planning for a safe future.

And this is despite a good dose of trust in the Divine and myself. It is despite knowing that I can't control the future, the present, or the past, and that surrender and going with the flow of the moment, with utmost acceptance, is the better way to live. I know from deep experience that in using my psychic and intuitive gifts, and communicating with the higher dimensions, I must take myself out of the equation, or I cannot receive guidance, simply because I have already given myself the answers I want to hear.

But in other areas of life, the same must apply - that all things are clearer and purer when we are not interjecting ourselves into the story. That we are open to receiving when we can let go of preconceived notions and judgments. To be open like a child and ask, "What are you…?" rather than having all the answers and filling every ounce of life, every breath of air, and every heartbeat with our wounds from the past, our fears, and our linear thinking.

Then, maybe freedom is a measure of becoming the observer, trusting deeply, and being able to let go of having to have things a certain way. Maybe learning to not interject ourselves into life's flow is the key to feeling utterly alive and receiving what is meant to be.

## Letting Go Of The Old

A new perception is always healthy. It shows evolution and brings a new truth that has evolved as well. Try to see your Spirit self as a flower or tree with constant new growth, a balance of the depletion of the old needing to be removed, making way for the new. We grow like they do; we blossom and are beautiful. Plants will stop giving energy to the old, giving it to the new, just as we should. When the flower has served its purpose, the plant will push it off or we must remove it. Give thanks for the beauty of our yesterdays as it withers and perishes, for it brings a renewed beauty and purpose for our today and every tomorrow. We are always making room for what needs to come into our lives. This is evolution. What was will never be again, nor shall it ever be the same. We make the choice to let go of the old and embrace the new. This is vulnerability and the only state we can grow within. Embrace it.

## Facing Our Traumas

I have the utmost respect, admiration, and appreciation for those who have chosen the healing journey. They possess an uncanny trust not only in themselves, but the Divine as well. They have chosen to go within, to find their courage, strength, and will, and allow their emotional pain and trauma to come forward to be healed. The darkness they face daily ensures their evolution with the allowance of what is meant to be. They accept the inner turmoil of seeing and feeling the memories from deep within come to light again, until they are not triggered by its presence. They have found a way to give it love and forgiveness when each layer comes back around. They know what it's like on the other side, never to be tortured by their demons again. They know what it means to learn self-mastery, and understand that each tomorrow may not be easy, but they face it head on. Heal well, journey well, former prisoners of the past.

## Overcoming Our Fears

There will always be those who are more than willing to spread fear by delusion. History shows us time and again that the masses are easier to control with fear. So, how do we not fall prey to these fear mongers? Quite simply, by trusting the Divine, seeking truth not delusion, and good old-fashioned research. They prey on the minds and uncertainties of those in search of answers. The ego will sift through information available to us, always ready to believe we are under attack from an unseen enemy. This is an ancient and deep-seeded belief passed down from generations long gone. It's up to us to lay these ill-gotten beliefs to rest by using discernment, truth, and trust. Our purpose, now, is to heal outdated ancestral beliefs and patterns, and learn to trust ourselves. Changing our mindset from fear to living in a state of love is the best way to overcome just about anything. As we all step into our authenticity, the paradigm shifts we need to make are readily available to us, but we need to allow our Spirit self to guide us, not the ego. Living in a state of love will certainly allow us to navigate these delusions safely and easily. It takes trust in yourself, your journey, the process, and the Divine. Keep it simple, and look for truth everywhere by listening to our Spirit, not our woundedness.

# Being in Judgement Of Others

The need to bring awareness to another's perceived shortcomings, faults, ideas, personal affairs, or any commentary on someone else and their journey, is nothing but our own ego acting out. When we belittle, berate, shame, or guilt another, whether it be to make ourselves feel bigger, or to make them feel smaller, we have given way for our wounded ego to dominate, and we are no longer coming from a place of love. This is a reflection on our own character, standing in judgement of that other person we wish to discredit. We have a responsibility to uplift and empower each other to be the very best version of ourselves, not tearing anyone else down. We must allow others to be who they are, regardless of whether we agree with their viewpoints or actions, and respect them and their journey. How others act, believe, or express themselves is a reflection on their relationship with themselves, and their journey and is none of our concern. When we live every aspect of our lives from the heart, we understand and accept this truth. Use this energy instead to focus on your own journey, doing the necessary work within yourself, allowing your authentic self to guide you with love.

# What To Do When We Are Triggered

Sometimes we get triggered so intensely that our emotions spike to violent heights. All we can do in those moments is to not act out, and temporarily disengage from the person who triggered us. They do not deserve our dumping the suppressed emotions of a lifetime of hurt onto them. These are our emotions, not theirs. As soon as possible, we need to withdraw to a safe space where we can feel our anger, sadness and whatever else comes up, and feel into the origins of our avalanche of emotions. Usually, it is our inner child who got triggered, and the wounds go back all the way to the abuse, rejection, and abandonment of our childhood. And so, we need to sit and exist within those emotions until we can release them, and give love and compassion to ourselves and to our inner child. Being triggered shows us what needs healing within us, and as such it is appropriate to give gratitude to those who triggered us, and provided the opportunity to do this deep healing. We may need to talk or set healthy boundaries once we are not in the triggered state anymore. But it is crucial not to get into a fight or argument, or make big decisions while we are under the influence of heightened emotions or notions for revenge. At this point, we would literally react with the immaturity of a hurt child. The question is not, "Why's this happening to me?" but "How can I learn and heal from this experience?" and "How can I use this trigger to change old, self-defeating patterns and grow?"

## Learning From Those We Encounter

We are both the teacher and the student, always learning from others, if we can be open to a higher truth. When we stop learning, our evolution has ceased and we have become static, allowing ourselves to live an egoic existence. We can always learn something from those we come in contact with, even if they show us how not to be in life, reminding us of a better way to live. Being open to learning from others is a maturity that is necessary if we want to grow and evolve. It offers a refreshing sense of freedom to be open and understanding that we don't know definitive truth. When we are triggered by others, we learn that there is healing we must allow. We can give gratitude that we were shown something about ourselves. That person just gave us an opportunity to heal and grow. Children show us how to be free, closer to our own Divinity, and that our natural state is love. The elders teach us much, based on their experiences in life. Some guide us on our journey, saving us from hardship and suffering. Don't ever believe that there is anyone above or below anyone. We are all unique and in different places on our respective journeys. When we can walk through this world with this state of mind, we see wonders and opportunities in our differences that enrich all of us.

# Building A New Foundation For The Future

Now that the shift is in full motion, what may happen during our lifetime? I see many with expectations that we will see drastic change soon in our favor. Quite honestly, we are building the foundation for the future. This means it will probably be drastic indeed, as we're picking through the rubble of what was, placing the right pieces for a stronger base to build upon. Don't expect to see major improvements on a grand scale in our lifetime, as the chaos of the destruction of the old, harmful systems takes place. Our responsibility is to plant seeds for those new to this journey, help guide them and each other, and to stay strong within our purposes. The outdated systems must fall to bring what serves Gaia and mankind. This is the darkness taking its last stand against the Age of Aquarius, and they will fight for their cause, just like us. The difference is that they will use everything at their disposal, as we have seen already. The lies, hatred, anger, and violence will become more prominent in their circles. All we need to do is stay the course, allow them to be them, and focus on our tasks at hand. Don't engage them, as this only gives them power. Remember, we don't have to accept their energy just because they want us to have it. Reject it and throw as much light as you possibly can back at them. We cannot allow ourselves to lower to their level of darkness. Keep shining your lights brightly for those in need. United we stand, divided we fall.

## Doing What We Came Here To Do

Most of us strive for an easy, abundant, spiritual life in which the Universe bends to our every wish, and in which we are permanently happy, safe, and free of pain and problems. We want to have things our way, find stability and permanence in what is familiar, and be in control. And yet during this shift on Earth, our bubbles are bursting, and the veils are being lifted. We are being upgraded to new frequencies, and the Universe appears to have little regard for our fantasies of how our life should be. We are being pushed to do deep inner healing work, and learn and grow at a rapid pace. Many experience anxiety, anger, grief, hopelessness, and sleepless nights. Our sense of reality and of ourselves is shifting. We are scared of the unknown, and of being outside of our comfort zone. We feel naked and vulnerable, and are faced with our lack of trust in ourselves and the Divine, having to learn much in a short amount of time. The Universe is trying to be as gentle as can be, but there is an urgency for us to evolve and reconnect with our Spirit. We did not come here just for ourselves, but also to be of assistance to others and help Mother Earth. It is time for us to allow the internal changes, roll up our sleeves, and do what needs to be done. There is a plan in place for our earthly life that the Divine holds. And we are being aligned with what we came here to do. Trust the changes that are unfolding.

# Why We Shy Away From Making Changes

Many of us would like to make changes in our lives for the better, yet we are unsure how to make these changes. What's holding you back? Fear? Not knowing the first step? Afraid of failing again? Perhaps it's not believing in yourself. Or maybe, you just don't have the drive because you've been in a dark place for too long. Regardless of the reasons, there is always a place to start. Give yourself permission to try something new. Our cellular self has been gridlocked within the comfort zone we created many years ago, and stepping out of that box terrifies us. Change is good. In fact, it's essential. Start with accepting that change must be made. Within you is the courage and strength you need. In fact, all you'll ever need is already within you. Talk it through with someone you trust. Make a physical list of what you'd like to do. Expand that list to why you should begin making changes. Expand it even further and explore within yourself why you have reservations about making changes. This is self-mastery at its core. Know why you aren't able to start something new. Spend time with all of this. You'll find much about yourself you may not have known, and you'll open yourself up to making the changes that you can make.

# Opinions Are The Lowest Form Of Knowledge

There will always be those who are critical of what we do, say, write, or believe. I thank them because it shows me how they feel about themselves. Their opinion regarding our efforts is a reflection of their relationship with themselves, and has absolutely nothing to do with us. They don't understand, and really don't care for the fact that we all are entitled to our beliefs without their persecution. Allow them to be as they are, even if they can't find it within themselves to allow us to be who we are. Don't take their criticism personal, don't give them the satisfaction of a response or reaction, and don't let them tear you down. Doing this will effectively take their perceived power away from them. Plato said, "Haven't you noticed that opinion without knowledge is always a poor thing?" which means that they formulate an opinion based upon an emotional response, without any knowledge of facts. In a more modern take, it has been said that opinion is the lowest form of knowledge. Stay true to your beliefs and yourself, until a higher truth presents itself. Be mindful of your own opinions and where they originate.

# Working With Traumatic Memories

We all have fears, and I personally know how they can paralyze us in an instant, leaving us short of breath and unable to function properly. All fears can be traced back to a single incident, perhaps a traumatic experience that shut us down. How can we overcome these traumatic memories that years later still stop us dead in our tracks? We face them head on. We don't confront them when they come forward. We embrace them with all the love we can and show them acceptance. It's self-defeating to get angry and reject our painful memories and emotions, much like we do with the parts of ourselves that we don't like. Admonishing them only drives them deeper within us. Showing them love will calm our cellular self. Find the root cause, the origin, and observe the experience through the Spirit, not the ego. See truth, not an egoic perception. Give the memory love and forgiveness and allow your cellular self to release the pain you feel. Sometimes, we can't find the root because it comes from a past life origin. It'll present itself in time, be patient. Like all traumatic experiences, our memories and emotions return in layers to be removed one at a time. When the memory no longer triggers us, we may consider it healed.

## The Natural Process Of Deep Healing

When we experience something traumatic or our feelings get hurt, we usually plummet into an abyss of emotional pain. There is a shock associated with losing our normal mode and falling headfirst into our own darkness. In this triggered emotional state, we easily blame, project our anger, and see what happened from a wounded perspective that is narrowed to seeing only our side of the story. We literally cannot see beyond our pain. Everything feels magnified in this internal place of despair, and we see ourselves as the victim.

Some may try to help us by trying to guide us out of this internal place of victimization and pain. But we must take our time here, and not rush anything, not override our emotions, and try to lift ourselves to a better place. We must process deeply, befriend our pain, and grieve what we have lost. We must embrace our anger and sadness, and let them find safe expressions. Then… when we have let ourselves thoroughly feel all of the internal messes, we can - in our own organic timing - turn a corner, and process what happened from a larger perspective that includes facts and the other side of the story. We can find compassion for others and ourselves.

With a clarity that was missing before, while we were going through the depth of our emotional pain, we can determine boundaries or actions that need to follow what happened.

Now, we are in the process of healing, regaining our power, and moving on.

But never ever deny yourself or another the right to completely fall apart, make absolutely no sense, and reel in emotional pain. We cannot save anyone from going deep in order to heal, as we all must, if we want to come out on the other side. We can be there and offer compassion, but healing has its own natural course, and looks different for each and every one of us. Honor what you feel, and trust that you will be okay.

To come "phoenix out of the ashes" is a devastating process that first has us destroyed, and then, finding our will and taking ownership of our life again, using what happened to us as fuel for our own growth and evolution. This is a true metamorphosis that needs to happen organically, with all stages allowed in their own way. There are no shortcuts to healing, and this we must accept.

Depending on the severity of what happened to us that triggered the emotional cascade, we may spend hours, days, months, or years in the emotional hole. While there is always the possibility of getting stuck in that dark place inside and in the victim role, we must trust ourselves, the healing process, and the Divine that something will prompt us when it is time to rise again. We will, eventually, be able to see beauty again and feel alive in a whole new way.

This is the journey into the unknown that is accompanied by a lot of rawness and vulnerability. We truly don't know who we will be when we come out of this alchemical process. This is why trust is so important on our journey, no matter what happens to us along the way. Our guides and angels, our Spirit, and Mother/Father God are always right there with us.

We may not be able to hear or feel them, especially if we are in survival mode or deep inside our own darkness, but we can, nonetheless, trust and know that we are being guided, and deeply cared for and loved. While this doesn't take our pain away, it helps immensely and lightens our load to not feel alone or abandoned. We know we can make it through with the help of the Divine.

## Our Trust Has To Be Earned

All too often we have trusted another, only to taste betrayal, and end up beating ourselves down for "not learning our lesson." Trust is a gift that we should reserve for those who can maintain honesty and accountability. By all means we need to trust, but it must be with discernment. Before you give the precious gift of trust to someone, feel their energy, study what they do, as opposed to what they say, and listen to how they speak about others and themselves. Give yourself permission to see beyond the façade and self-promoted image of another. How do you feel in their presence? Do you feel stifled, shamed, and small or supported, truly seen, and appreciated for who you are? Do they take your energy and dump on you, or is it a mutually beneficial exchange? Many with low self-esteem feel that they owe others their lives. We tend to see the light in everyone but ourselves, and forget to see the reality of their earthly self for what it is. We prefer our fantasy of who we want them to be over the honest reality, and having to make some hard choices. When we trust someone, we give them access to our very essence. Trust your gut instincts. Spend time with someone before you gift them with an opportunity to hurt you and take advantage of you. Trust yourself. Our hearts are sacred and must be protected, as is with all that we hold sacred.

## Gratitude For Learning Our Lessons

We cannot carry guilt and shame for the lessons we have learned, or how we had to learn them. It took lifetimes of living before we could come to a place where we could learn them in the here and now. This is a self-sabotaging thought process, and we need to change it to self-love and compassion. Embrace what you learned and turn it to wisdom, with grace. Allow yourself to heal through self-forgiveness and unconditional love, with understanding and mercy. Give gratitude for the growth you have experienced through the process. Learn to be thankful for who you were. For it is because of who you we were then that you are the person you are today.

## The Fruits Of Our Inner Work

Doing the inner work and allowing our evolution leads us to feeling so secure in ourselves, trusting so deeply that we don't need to run, hide, please, or enable others. We are no longer afraid of life, and no longer feel the need to trade our power for a sense of safety. This is freedom.

# The Gifts of Vulnerability

Vulnerability is a necessary state on our spiritual and awakening journeys. It brings us room for expansion, allows us to be in the moment, and leads to the very freedom we all desire and need in our life. Being vulnerable means we have everywhere to go, with the understanding that we are the ones limiting ourselves on our journey. An unfortunate side effect is we have no clue where we belong, but does anyone truly know where we are meant to be? We will never know until we arrive there, where we feel safe, respected, wanted, loved, and home. There, we may find our soul tribe, perhaps the one we are meant to be with, or maybe, the isolation we need at that time. We won't even know what it feels like until we have the realization that we finally made it. That will be given in time, as we become accustomed to the new comfort felt once the search has ended. Until that time comes, we must remain steadfast in our uncomfortableness, with trust and knowing that we are always exactly where we are meant to be on our journey.

# Healing Our Inner Child

We cannot heal or advance in our evolution without healing our inner child. Our inner child holds the key to our freedom, creativity, authenticity, and original connection with our own Spirit and God. Every adult has an inner child as part of their psyche, and for most people they are hiding within, feeling overlooked, neglected, and unloved. With patience, compassion, and love we must find a way to reconnect with our inner youngling, and regain their trust. Recovering, healing, and integrating this inner child is at the core of self-love. Usually, they are stuck at the age when we experienced heavy traumas in childhood, and when we were so stifled, abandoned or abused that this part of ourselves split off and went into hiding. This child living within us, still, needs the nourishment, love, and acceptance that we didn't get when we were young - just that now they need this from us. In return for helping them heal their wounds, traumas, and fears, and including them lovingly into our daily lives, they will give us a sense of wholeness and feeling alive. They will rekindle our playfulness and creativity, and reconnect us with our intuition, spiritual gifts, and communication with God. Heal the inner child and they will set the adult free.

# The Basis For Our Relationships

Your relationship with yourself is the most important one you have, and all others are based on this fact. There must be love of the self before there can be love for others, and the same is true with respect, trust, and emotional availability. If we cannot respect and trust ourselves, we cannot offer it to others. We have to heal emotionally from our past traumas and pains, before we can allow someone access to us emotionally, or be there for someone else on an emotional level. We have to know who we are at a deep level before we can meet someone deep within themselves. To be able to love someone unconditionally, we have to be able to love ourselves first. We must be honest with ourselves and who we are, before we can see honesty in them, and allow ourselves to accept them for who they are without judgment. There is a natural flow between giving and receiving with grace and mercy that exists in equal measure, and we must allow ourselves to receive with that same grace and mercy as we give. We must be healed and balanced enough, becoming the best possible mate, before we are ready for the best mate possible for us. When you are both healed, it will happen as it is meant to, when it is meant to. Allow the flow to come naturally, without looking, for if it is meant to be, it will be.

## Learning To Like Ourselves Again

Few things are more crippling to our spiritual, mental, and physical wellbeing than not forgiving ourselves. Most of us hold deep resentments toward ourselves for past mistakes, perceived failures, and for not living up to our own and other people's perfectionistic expectations. We hide these dark pockets of unforgiveness deep inside, below our surface smiles, stoic tendencies, and conditioned responses.

Most of us have never actually liked ourselves, and to this day, treat ourselves with silent condemnation and harsh criticism, shaming ourselves into the ground on a daily basis. We continue to hurt ourselves, and deepen our childhood wounds of feeling unworthy, not good enough, and not trusting ourselves. Yet, we don't realize that what we disliked and could not relate with is who we became though a lifetime of being in survival mode and being molded into someone we are not.

These destructive cellular patterns and habits that have been passed down through the generations ensured that we would not be our authentic selves, but tamed and tainted as the ones in our lineage before us. We took the projections of others as reality, and hated ourselves for what they saw in us, not knowing that their perceptions and projections were a reflection of them, and not of us.

It takes finding our will and doing the inner work of deep emotional healing to be able to break the cycle of self-shaming and punishment. We must allow honesty and awareness, and with compassion and love for ourselves, and what we have been through, peel away the layers of anger, judgment, and self-rejection. We may need to clean things up and make amends to those we have hurt. But most of all, we must set things right with ourselves, and forgive ourselves.

We are indeed deserving of our own respect, support, and unconditional acceptance. And as we do the inner work of excavating the precious self that we are, and embracing our authenticity, we will find that we actually like who we are. We are able to, finally, give ourselves the love and approval that we have been seeking all our lives.

## Letting Go Of Expectations

Expectations are a predetermined outcome. We all have wants and needs, but when we become fixated on a very particular outcome, we are, in fact, trying to manipulate the Universe to our will. This is a major block on our journey. By only seeing one possible ending, we negate all other options, some for our highest good. This is clear evidence that we need to keep our options open to receive what is for our highest good. Our Spirit self will always guide us to what is best for our 3D self. We eventually end up robbing ourselves of conscious evolution on our chosen path. We can, however, open ourselves to allow Divine guidance by asking for what will propel us on our journey. This is grace at its finest understanding. Expectations will only leave us with a sense of disappointment, and may become toxic to us on many levels. Remove the block, allow what you've contracted for, and believe that you will always be provided for. Like the song says, "… You can't always get what you want, but if you try sometime, you'll find, you get what you need…" We will always be given exactly what we need. Trust yourself, your journey, the process, and God.

## The Bridge Will Appear

Most of us are afraid of success, not of failure. We often say, "I can't" and what we really mean is, "I won't." This puts a dead stop to forward movement. Whether it is fear, self-doubt, or overwhelm that stops us from moving forward, we believe that we lack the strength to face a situation and find a way through it. To say, "I can't" precludes that we could take baby steps and breathe our way through our fears, and that the bridge will appear as we trust the Universe to hold and guide us. Being clear that we don't want to do something can be a healthy boundary, or quitting what isn't working, a wise and self-loving decision. But saying to yourself that you "can't" is to limit yourself, your creativity and innovativeness, and to keep yourself stuck in your comfort zone. There is always a way. Things are never just black and white, all or nothing. Don't limit yourself and keep yourself small. You are a Child of Light and not bound by the confines of the 3D world. You do not need to know "how" before you take the first step. Find your courage, trust yourself, and allow the adventure of life to unfold. You can indeed – if you believe in yourself.

## Creating New References As We Evolve

Since we are in a constant state of evolution, we cannot find solutions for our problems or issues with the same mentality we have always used. Now that we are beyond our yesterdays, we need to find new solutions as the old references are no longer relevant. This means we need to have a different mindset and new tools in our arsenal in which we see unique answers. Step beyond what we have always perceived to be truth, as our truth has evolved, as well. We've grown, learned, and healed past the old, outdated methods we have become accustomed to. Evolution also brings new problems and issues which will also need a different mindset to overcome. This will take a conscious effort to realize our old patterns and beliefs are a part of who we were, not who we are now. Taking steps to bring the changes we need to keep up with our evolution will propel us to new heights and new ways necessary to maintain this evolution. You already have the answers within you. Allow your guides to do their part, simply by listening with your heart, and allowing this new mentality to formulate. Give them the trust and respect they deserve, and watch your life change in many ways on many levels.

# Going Within

When we are truly in touch with our own Divinity, we have surrendered ourselves, and our authentic selves will hear, see, and feel a higher consciousness. For all this to take place we must transcend the ways of the 3D, and evolve beyond what we thought we knew. You have the courage, strength, and wisdom of lifetimes within you making all this possible for you. Find them. Go deep within. You will never find what you are looking for out there. Nor is there any need to believe that you need someone else to do it for you because you aren't capable or lack trust in yourself. You are indeed quite capable on your own if you just trust yourself, your journey, the process, and God, allowing total surrender of your perceived control. Love yourself enough to abandon the old self-defeating patterns and beliefs that you were taught. Allow your journey to be what it is meant to be, and step into the Age of Knowing.

# The Celestial Consciousness Of Mother Earth

Most human beings are unaware of the incredibly deep interconnectedness we have with Mother Earth, with every breath and every heartbeat, and how completely our existence depends on her. Our planet is a living being, a celestial Spirit with a consciousness. She has thoughts and emotions, and she has needs.

Her consciousness has to evolve just as humans do, and she is right in the middle of a crucial metamorphosis, an ascension process to a higher frequency. Just as we do, she has much emotional and physical healing to do in this transition. And just as many of us, Mother Earth has sufficiently evolved to no longer tolerate abusive, exploiting behavior toward her. The elemental and Native earth spirits are pushing back as much as our planet is.

She is showing us right now, by the way of natural disasters, that she is incapable of taking any further disrespect and destruction towards her. Humanity would be wise to heed her warnings and messages, as she has demonstrated that her powers can be just as destructive as that of humanity, if not more.

Many lightworkers have come here at this time to assist and help usher in the new world. Human life is changing in ways that we could not have foreseen, and it will have to adjust to the new frequencies, and the needs of our planet. A Divine plan is unfolding, and the current human crisis is a continuing stage of the shift. The old ways have to crumble before the new can emerge. We are called to trust that we will be okay as long as we remain open to the changes. If we fight them, and hang onto our old ways of thinking and acting, we will lose the battle.

Mother Earth needs our help, now more than ever. Every time we go out in nature and extend loving energy, she benefits. When we admire her beauty, tend to plants, pick up trash, sing to the river, set out a water dish for wild animals, or commune with the fae world, we bring peace to her. When we chose thoughtfulness towards the environment, reducing toxins, we help ease her burdens. Every time we work with our crystals and gemstones, which are a part of her consciousness, they not only help us heal, but also return that healing energy to her. With awareness, there is much that we can do to help the consciousness of our beloved planet survive what humanity has done to her, and help her find her balance again.

## Don't Force Your Healing

Within the midst of a transition from one phase to the next, we may experience grieving, as we have released a part of us that is no longer necessary for our evolution. Oftentimes, we find that we need to let go of old patterns and beliefs that are making this transition more difficult. Stay the course and allow this to be as it's meant to be. Don't try to force any further healing or emotional adjustments. This has purpose beyond our understanding. When we try to force our healing, we don't allow the organic flow within, creating unnecessary struggles for ourselves. We had an old saying where I used to work, "If it aren't broke, don't fix it…" You're not broke, so there's nothing to fix. Allowance. Patience. Perseverance. Let it be organic because the minute you inject yourself into the story, you've created a block. This is making room for what is best for our highest good, by releasing what no longer serves us. Don't try to control what you're experiencing because you can't. Allow the organic flow to come. Remember, everything is temporary, and the next layer of healing will visit again, but now you have a reference point, making it easier than the last layer.

# From Self-Loathing To Self-Love

One of the patterns of my former self and most self-defeating, was making myself small. Regardless of whether it was because I felt belittled, intimidated, or any other reason I could come up with, I was giving my power away. Quite the price to pay for my own insecurities. I would shrink back into some form of a child, retreating to the comfort of my own personal shame. Oh, the pain I felt inside because I felt weak, often coming to words of self-hatred. I condemned myself to being something incredibly less than what I believed myself to be. One day, I absolutely couldn't stand this part of me and made my stand. I vowed to never allow myself to be made to feel small and denigrated. I found my inner strength and courage, and stood up to myself, no one else. Enough was enough and I hit that Popeye syndrome, "I've had all I can stands, cause I can't stands no more." I've never looked back since I decided to end the cycle of self-abuse I had become so accustomed to. I ended the pity parties of self-loathing, and made the decision to stand tall within. That was many years ago. Through this journey, I've found self-love and respect, with a healthy dose of inner boundaries and pride. This mindset wasn't easy, but I made that conscious decision to regain my dignity, and promised to live from the heart in every aspect of my life. You have this within you. Go deep and find it. Change your perspective, change your life.

## Staying True To Our Journey

How are we supposed to live in a world filled with hatred, anger, rage, and entitlement? Simply by remembering our happiness is a choice we make daily. The outer world is something we must be aware of, but we don't have to absorb that energy. We stay true to ourselves and our journey. We shine our light brightly, sending it out over all we come in contact with. We keep spreading our love, perhaps with a smile for a stranger. We remember the path that lays before us, and we focus on that. We uplift each other with kindness. What others think of us is a reflection of their relationship with themselves, and has nothing to do with us, so we don't take it personal. We don't engage in their anger, rage, and hatred. We allow them to be who they are, as they have their path before them, as well. We stay within the mindset of living from the heart in every aspect of our lives. We trust the Divine, knowing this is the shift in progress, and we can't possibly fathom what is going on in their bigger picture. We have to trust ourselves deeply and hold our journeys closer to our hearts. Finally, don't give into the fears they want us to have. Stay the course of your path, remain calm, and know God never abandons us.

# Healing Hurtful Projections from Childhood

We all grew up with projections of guilt and shame from just about everyone we knew at some point. The most damaging, though, came from our guardians. We had to trust them because they were our role models, the very ones who we looked up to for love and support. So, how do we heal those damaging words that keep echoing through our adult lives? We forgive them, however many times it takes to not be triggered. We call our inner child forward, giving them all the love we can, with reassurance. We show the inner woundedness that we are not those hateful words. We explain how our guardians were raised, without justifying their behavior. When those words haunt us, we hold our inner child close, telling them, "You're okay…" over and over. We become the parents we needed then, with an abundance of nurturing and more forgiveness. We give them the acceptance they didn't find, with words of encouragement that they won't be hurt anymore. We show them who we are now and how much we've grown from those days, showing them the beauty we have become. Heal the inner child and they will show the adult self, freedom. Given the chance, they will show us where we need to heal the most. We empower them with all the love we can give them.

## The Necessity For Humility

Knowing our truth is essential on our awakening journey. This is self-mastery at its core, as we must know ourselves on the deepest level possible for today. Our perception is ours and we must maintain grace within it. Believing our truth is absolute is a major block to our evolution, as there is no possible way for our truth to evolve as we do. Being locked into our beliefs eliminates any chance of growth or learning. Everyone and everything is teaching us something, but if we're not allowing ourselves to learn, then we're stuck within a status quo, and there is no forward and upward movement. Indeed, God is within us, but this does not make us God, or even a god. Humility and grace help us to quell the voice of our woundedness which insists we be perfect. We really need to accept the fact that we know nothing to very little of this life, and we can't possibly have all the answers. If we hold this belief in superiority, then we are injecting ourselves into everything, making it about us, and we have totally missed truth right in front of us. A healthy sense of humility will ensure that we are open to learning and growing, allowing life to touch us.

# Setting Healthy Boundaries

Setting healthy boundaries does not need to become a battle ground or a confrontation. We need to set healthy boundaries for ourselves to let others know it is not okay for them to treat us in an undeserving manner, or put us in any situation we do not feel comfortable within. It is simply us, speaking our truth from a place of love. We don't have to speak in such a manner as to make another feel defensive, but if they become defensive, it is because they have been triggered. Their trigger has nothing to do with us, as it is something within them that needs to be healed. We deserve respect and understanding, even if they don't understand. Setting healthy boundaries brings us freedom within our journey with an ability to feel peace. When others don't abide by the boundaries we have set, we can either choose to keep repeating ourselves or remove ourselves from their energy, which may mean we need to thank them for their part on our journey with love and move on. Love and respect yourself enough to speak your truth from the heart, and live with an inner peace you deserve.

# Preserving Our Sovereignty In Love Relationships

When we are in an intimate long-term relationship with another, it can feel like they are our other half, the one who completes us. This romantic notion may work while everything is going our way, and our life together is new. But when things get difficult within the dynamics of the relationship, toxic patterns get projected, or life throws hardships at us, it is not helpful to cling to another as an integral part of ourselves. This level of codependence – depending on another for our life, livelihood, and identity - has brought us immense heartbreak and suffering, lifetime after lifetime.

Trying to exchange the self that we didn't like for one that seems better, by becoming a part of someone else, doesn't work. If we were truly a part of another, and they were a part of our being, then we would be justified in changing them into who we need them to be. Their autonomy would be frustrating to us because they would always slip out of our grip of control, and against all our attempts to protect them, be touched by the harshness of life.

While the Oneness certainly exists in the higher realms of the Divine, we are not all one, here, on this planet. This goes also for our soul mate, twin flame, or beloved over many lifetimes. While our Spirits may have known each other for eons, we are on individual journeys, with the divinely given right to our own sovereignty. We can share our joys and pains, cry and heal in each other's arms, and embrace each other with the purest love that our hearts hold. But we cannot reduce ourselves to half a being, adding the other to our self to feel whole, as this is an illusion that will, in time, cause us immense suffering.

Traditionally, women were conditioned to see themselves as a part of the man they married, and to give up their own identity as symbolized by taking his name. He was her protector and provider, and she his possession, in undying loyalty to him. While most of us have moved far beyond these archaic customs of the patriarchal era, we all carry the remnants of our conditioning in our bones.

Hollywood movies have done their own share of brainwashing with the ideal of a romance so strong that two halves become one, each sacrificing their selves to their perceived oneness. But what becomes of the remaining half when the other walks away, or becomes ill and passes from their earthly existence? How are we to be able to continue living if our partner really was half of who we are? This romantic idealism is often the cause that the one surviving the other can never accept that their partner is no longer with them in the physical. Many cannot, in their lifetime, find their way back to their own selfhood. If most of our self really dies with the other, then what are we left with but an empty shell?

It is of absolute importance for a healthy relationship that we have our own identity, authenticity, and inner freedom. It is unhealthy to become a part of someone else, and abandon our own needs and ways of living our life. This doesn't mean that we don't compromise, and both make concessions in the relationship, learning to be flexible and patient with each other. But we cannot give up our sovereignty as a being without paying a heavy price.

There truly is no historic precedent for what a healthy relationship looks like. We are the pioneers of a new way of living that doesn't sacrifice one for another. Honoring all involved, with their highest good always at heart, we are witnessing to each other's journeys, with the love and respect for our individuality that we are all deserving.

# Revisiting Our Experiences in Gratitude

We write our life story as we live it. Some chapters we'd just as soon forget, some chapters we wish were never written, and then there are those chapters we cherish. But the fact remains that it's our story and no one else's. Regardless of how painful some chapters are, we need to feel an enormous amount of accomplishment. Through those times we'd rather forget, we learned about life, ourselves, and others. Those chapters brought us wisdom, knowledge, strength, and many other wonderful qualities about ourselves that were quite necessary to write our stories of every tomorrow. Without those experiences we would never be able to step out of our comfort zone to learn, heal, and grow. Now is the time to go back and revisit some of those things we'd rather forget. Look how far you've come since then. Just because a time in our life and its events were painful, doesn't mean they haven't helped shape us into who we are now. See how valuable those experiences are now. You always started a new chapter being a much different person than the last one written. While you're revisiting it again, heal the pains and traumas, and every subsequent experience will be much different. Look how you've learned, grown, and healed. Well, go on! Thank yourself for those pains and traumas. They made you who you are.

## Forgiving Ourselves For Hurting Others

We can't make up for our broken yesterdays, but we can and we must heal them. We can't make the past right, but we can, and we must make our today right within us. Forgive yourself for what was and ask forgiveness from those we have wronged, even if it was with intent. The realization of knowing our erroneous ways will begin the healing process, but we must stop beating ourselves up for what has been done. We are not that person anymore, so we cannot live in that past, blaming and shaming ourselves for our transgressions. We must heal deep within what caused us to become who we were, and we must release the past through healing the traumas and pains that we felt and projected onto others. Please remember that everything happens as it is meant to, so find within you the courage and strength to face the truth of those yesterdays, with the understanding that it's in the past and we cannot stay there. Accept your part during it all, correct for today all that you can, but above all, stop the self-inflicted suffering for what was. Make today right within yourself and keep doing that for every today that you live. Be loving and compassionate with yourself and allow the healing to take place for yourself and those you have hurt.

# Finding Our Own Truth

One of the disadvantages of a lifetime of looking outside of ourselves for truth, answers, and approval is that we lose touch with who we are and what our truth is. Now, we must learn to trust ourselves again, cultivate and heed our intuition, and practice discernment. We may have given our power away in the past, and suspended disbelief all too quickly. Many on a spiritual journey have arranged their lives and belief systems around a certain book or teacher, without ever really questioning the assumed status of absolute truth that their words were given. Often, the practice of these teachings and associated culture became the box we lived within. Now, it is time to let go of what no longer serves our highest good and give gratitude for our spiritual stepping-stones. Dogma has no place on our journey and any idols we previously held onto must fall. If we want to evolve, we have to question everything we believe we know, allowing a change in perspective and awareness. We are limitless Beings. The knowledge and wisdom that we have been seeking out there is already within us. Learn to trust yourself and find your truth – not someone else's - but your truth.

## When The Universe Closes Doors On Us

There are times in our lives when the Universe closes one door after another. Whatever we are attempting isn't going anywhere, and despite all our efforts, our life as it was, is falling apart. This can be frustrating and even depressing, as we usually have no clue as to what is going on, and why nothing we attempt is working.

When we notice that we are in such a phase of many doors closing on us, step back. Don't try to force anything. The Divine has just stepped in, and is moving us on our journey to where we need to be for our highest good. Trust this process. We are in a major transition from one phase of our lives to another. There is purpose to this beyond what we can see. While the unknown is usually uncomfortable for us, as human beings, this is where trust and patience are essential. This phase is not the end-all. It's like being in a darkened hallway where we cannot see where we are going.

Step closer to your Spirit, your guides, and the Divine Mother/Father. They've got you. You are not lost just because you cannot see the path ahead of you. As we allow this spaciousness, the flow that the Universe has set in motion will carry us to where we need to be. A few months from now, or a year from now, our lives will look very different.

Every time there is a phase in our lives where many doors close, it is followed by a phase purging the old from our lives. This can be painful, depending on how much we resist the changes. Trust, willingness, and acceptance will make everything a lot easier and gentler. At some point, the transition will be completed and the new brought into our lives.

The timing is not up to us. So, we might as well accept our loss of control, and enjoy each phase with curiosity, and let the Universe do its magic. The less we resist, the smoother the transition will be. The level of trust we can give to the Divine will determine how much we can allow ourselves to release the old that is no longer serving our highest good and embrace what is meant to be.

## Let Life Touch You

Break free from the conditioning, the smallness, the silence. Deep inside, underneath all the shoulds and musts that came from other people's projections, is the raw, pure essence of who you are in your Spirit form. Open yourself to the life that is waiting to be lived by you. Let it come forward and find its natural expression. Let life touch you. Be brave. Trust that you will not fall. Stumble, yes, and tumble at times. But always helped by the Divine. Always.

## When It's Time To Let People Go

The more we evolve and reconnect with our Divinity, the more some people will feel threatened by who we are. They cannot understand the place we are coming from, and all that it took for us to get here. They will project their anger, fears, guilt, and other unprocessed emotions onto us. They will see all of their darkness in us, accusing us of exactly what they are doing. The closer the relationship with that person, the more we feel hurt. But the truth is that there is no reason for us to take their energy, words, and behaviors. None of their actions and reactions have anything to do with us, being a reflection of their relationship with themselves. We owe it to ourselves to act from self-love and set healthy boundaries. We do not owe them anything, and we do not need to take the burden that they are unloading. Many of us grew up being everyone's doormat, and being dumped upon by those around us, while we were looking for validation and acceptance. It is time for us to change these patterns, say goodbye to the victim role, and to stand tall in our own truth. We never apologize for who we are, or try to change ourselves to fit other people's expectations or demands. If we have outgrown people, and they cannot accept who we are, then it may be time to let them go. Allow others to be who they are and move on. We must honor who we are, and nurture and protect our heart and sacred energy.

# Opportunity To Learn, Grow, and Heal

When we feel that we must keep perpetuating an experience, we become mired down and stuck within recreating that experience, unable to move beyond it. This serves only to keep us in the past and inside an illusion we are creating. There is, at this point, no forward movement. Spirituality is not about an experience but rather about embracing trust and allowing what is meant to be. As we believe we can control our spirituality, we create our own block, remaining stagnant and unable to evolve. Move beyond the belief that spirituality is an experience, knowing that it is a lifelong series of experiences meant to bring opportunity to learn, grow, and heal. Let go of the illusions that we created by becoming the observer, and giving ourselves permission to see truth outside of our own perspective. Create an inner environment to succeed within, not an illusion to keep reliving.

# The Promise Of A New Way, A New Day

From an awakening perspective, the common need right now is for love, mercy, grace, and forgiveness. Thoughts of vengeance, hatred, and despise only add fuel to the darkness wreaking this havoc in our world. We must spread love, our own Christ Conscious energy, and hope. We all must trust the shift process put before us, with acceptance of what is meant to be. There is purpose beyond our understanding, and this, we must accept. Allow love to flow from the heart unconditionally to raise Mother Earth's vibration as she is also under attack. Raise your voice with love, not condemnation, fear, or any other negativity. This is how we make a difference, and this is how we change the world. By all means, recognize the plight of those directly affected, but send them what they need the most. Love. Hope. Grace. Mercy. From this chaos the foundation we have been building will begin to take form, and The New Way, The New Day, as promised, will rise from the ashes. Shine your light for those in need, and become the beacon they seek.

# Without Trust There Can Be No Evolution

I see many of us entering an unprecedented phase of extreme vulnerability. Not only is this very uncomfortable, it leaves us not knowing what's going on, or what our next step is. Regardless of how off we feel, we absolutely must bring even more trust into our journeys. We can't see the big picture, and having been taught as kids how to try and control our lives, we have to understand that we simply can't. This is what's bringing suffering and other problems into our lives. We can't fight what is coming, propelling us awkwardly into our evolution. Many of us are interjecting ourselves into the stories the Universe has written; by believing we have to know and understand everything, with suppositions, assumptions, and opinions without true facts. This is counterproductive and can be quite toxic to us. This fear of the unknown can be a major block in many aspects of our lives. Without trust there can be no evolution. Since we basically have tunnel vision, we can only see from our perception, which is mostly guided by the 3D self. Allow what is meant to be and bring even more trust into your life and your journey. I can't stress the importance of this enough. Keep it simple, my friends. There are plans in place for all of us. We simply have to trust in the Divine and ourselves. Trust yourself, trust your journey, trust the process, and trust God. This is how we surrender our illusory control.

## The Ride Of Our Lives

These are not easy times as the shift on Earth progresses. We are all called, prompted, and forced to change. We cannot hold on to the comfortable, the safe, and lukewarm any longer, and keep defending our limited perception and previous identity. We cannot avoid self-awareness and deep honesty with ourselves anymore. The things we haven't healed are coming up for healing now, and we must break the habits of hiding and running from our emotions, and face them head on with compassion, patience, and love. We are falling apart and being put together anew by the Universe. The less we fight it, using old ideas to measure and interpret what is happening to us, the easier our evolution will be. We are not in control anymore, and while this may seem scary, we must learn to allow these changes to happen within us, and trust ourselves, our Spirit's guidance, the process, and Mother/Father God. We have to remember that we did not come here at this time to live a comfortable, soft, spiritual life. We came here to heal and awaken, and to assist humanity and Mother Earth through this historically unprecedented transformation. We are truly in for the ride of our lives.

## Labor Of Love

Freedom and happiness are incredibly subjective to our perception of ourselves. Most of us have never really liked ourselves. Through our childhood conditioning, we became who we were molded to be, instead of who we really are. Our authenticity was stifled, and so was our creative expression of the self. We have felt unfree for so long that we don't remember how to keep it simple and just enjoy the moment. We don't remember how it feels to be content with ourselves, instead of trying to live up to the impossible expectations we set for ourselves, adding to our sense of unworthiness, and not measuring up. But within us is all we need - to live from the heart a life of moment-to-moment gratitude, acceptance, personal freedom, and happiness. Our labor of love is healing ourselves and changing the old patterns so we can be free. We are loving ourselves back to life and finally finding acceptance for the beautiful being that we are, and always have been.

## People Come And Go In Our Lives

People come into our lives for a reason, a season, or a lifetime. Some will bring lessons, blessings, and some will be both. Many will leave a profound impact on your journey, some good, some indifferent, and some will bring you trauma. Regardless, they are a player in an experience you need to further your evolution. Some we welcome with love, some leave us with a familiar feeling of, "What just happened?" and others we will love to see leave. The majority of them will not be on our journey very long because they cannot go where we are going. Very few will actually be a part of our journey long term, and some will become our closest friend and confidant. Nonetheless, when their part on our journey is over, we need to thank them with love, even for the pain they brought. They came into our lives at precisely the right moment, and brought the exact experience we needed at that time. Let go of the attachments you had with them, allow yourself to learn, heal, and grow from the shared experience, and quietly move on, always, and in all ways, with love.

## We Are Never Finished

At what point do we consider that we have done enough healing, or have become "enlightened" and there is nothing more we need to do to evolve? Never. Healing and evolution are a constant and a never-ending process. If we give into complacency from the egoic suggestion of finality, then we have been deceived by it. There will always be more to do. There will always be more to learn. There will always be more to heal. We cannot allow ourselves to believe that we can go no farther. This is a self-imposed limitation to believe we have completed all there is to accomplish. Anyone who has ever mastered their trade or profession understands there is always one more step to improve upon, and simply won't allow themselves to believe that they are ever finished. Once we have made the strides to accomplish a task there will always be another waiting for us.

## The Hardships That Drive Our Evolution

I truly don't believe that our lives on a journey of conscious awareness were meant to be easy or simple. Where would we draw inspiration in a mundane world of status quo? Where would we find balance through a life of mediocrity? Where would we have opportunity to learn, heal, and grow in a world of sleep? I admit, there are many days when I cry uncle in the midst of difficulty. In all honesty, I would endure all I have, to be the person I have become. I'd endure the hardships of my childhood, the stroke, the countless mistakes I have learned from and am still learning from. I will always give gratitude for those rough days. We had a saying where I used to work, "You gotta have bad days to make the good days better." I remember the first time I heard that. I realized I was working with a bunch of blue-collar philosophers, most of them Vietnam veterans. They went through the worst life could offer and found some modicum of inner peace. They taught me much about life, and I always listened. Be thankful for the rough times, for without them, none of us would be who we are today.

# Taking Steps Toward Our Dreams

What inspires you? What is the passion that drives you? More importantly, are you living your passion? If not, are you able to make strides in your life toward living that dream? Our dreams, regardless of how farfetched, can be achieved in some fashion. Perhaps a larger forward movement isn't possible yet. But there is always a way to find some tangible way to bring even the smallest amount of your desired reality into your journey. Are you using all your resources, or do you fear the change? Most of us fear success because we've never known it on a grander scale, but we're all adapt at living within the comfort zone we created years ago. What have you got to lose? Keep trying. Failure doesn't exist until we admit defeat and give up. Edison tried approximately a thousand times to invent the lightbulb before he found it working. We learn from our non-success more than our success. Keep learning and keep the dream alive.

## Spiritual Wake-Up Call

The Divine, our Spirit, ancestors, and angels are always here to assist us, as we navigate whatever journey we are currently on. Always, and in all ways. But if you're waiting on them to complete your tasks for you, then you cannot possibly evolve. If you're not doing the inner work for yourself, then they will sit and wait tirelessly for you to get up off your duff. They have brought you many opportunities to further your evolution, but if you don't take an active role, then it's an exercise in futility for all involved. Although they will never abandon you, without the action you need to take, you are abandoning them. This means that where you are is where you'll stay, as the status quo will never bring forward movement. Get up, climb out of your self-neglect, and make something happen. It's truly up to you where your journey goes. They'll be waiting in the next life, just as they are now.

# The Roller Coaster Ride Of Life

What happens within our cellular self when we give gratitude? It sparks an awareness of beauty and the beginning of a new and prosperous perspective. We start to feel alive again because this belief begins to free us from the darkness we have become. Perhaps we've been down for so long that all we feel is negativity. We go deep into our darkness as it's the only way to our light, taming the dark within to bring a much-needed balance. As we endure this emotional pain, we honor what we feel. We don't need to understand or define it, just allow it to come to the front. We don't need to become it either. We exist, for a time, allowing whatever is deep within to present itself. When it has, we have definition, perhaps without words, perhaps just a respect for it, knowing it has purpose. Trying to understand everything is a control mechanism. We can't possibly understand it all, as much of it is from the Spirit self, not the 3D self. Our Spirit is evolving, and so much of what is unknown is being healed from past lifetimes. When life becomes a roller coaster ride, keep your arms and legs inside the ride at all times, until it comes to a complete stop, and enjoy your stay on Earth.

## Harm No One

Every choice we make will undoubtedly affect the lives of others. Every decision we make is a statement about who we are. There will always be consequences for the choices and decisions we make. By all means we must do as we need in our personal life, while understanding those choices and decisions may have a direct and profound impact upon others. This is but one of the many fine lines we walk on any journey. We will have our own reasons for the choices and decisions we make. Others will always have their decisions to make for themselves, based on their personal life and what is best for them in response. Sometimes we will alienate those we love, but it must be understood that their decisions are not to be taken personally by us. Unfortunately, there may be collateral damage. Always be aware of the impact you create on the lives of others. Do as you need for your highest good, but harm no one.

## Breathe Before You Act

Before you react, take three deep breaths. This gives you time to stop your current thought process. It could also mean the difference between doing something you'll regret for the rest of your life, and grace. That three second window is all we need to allow the Spirit self to step in, and save us from egoic folly and a shattered experience. Breathe again. This one allows us to realize we're about to make a big mistake. This response comes from our authentic self, and is different from the reaction of our wounded ego. Our guides and Spirit will do all they can to help us, but we also have to make that a conscious effort and choice. This will pull us out of the rage and anger that our ego loves to react with. That one extra breath pulls us back to our center: the heart, back to our Spirit self. Learn to take those breaths and save yourself from regret, guilt, and self-shame, possibly destroying the rest of your life. Breathe… and breathe again… you'll be glad you did.

# The Adventure Of Our Life

Some of us wrote some pretty wild stories for our lifetime, with many plot twists and sudden surprises. Personally, I sometimes wonder what I was drinking when I signed those contracts before I incarnated. How are you navigating what you don't understand? Somewhere down the line in this lifetime, I must have misplaced the life manual they gave us, unless there just isn't one. A different perception if I may. Within all the twists and turns of our lives are wonderful opportunities to learn to adapt to what life brings us. That ability allows us to be guided by our angels, ancestors, and guides, given that we have the ability to trust. Our trust in the Divine and ourselves is the easiest way to navigate whatever surprises life has in store for us. Think of it as an adventure instead of a pain in the proverbial backside. An adventure brings us so much more opportunity than trying to fight what we don't like. Accept the truth that whatever has happened has purpose and see it as opportunities to learn, heal, and grow. Stop asking, "Why is this happening to me?" and give gratitude for chances to evolve.

# The Evolution Of Our Spirit

A new Spirit emerges, awaiting an opportunity to incarnate into form. It has no reference points for any thought, emotions, or experience. It is pure in its energy form with no understanding of what life is about. It spends many lifetimes accumulating knowledge, wisdom, and experiences. It understands the best and worst any life form could witness and experience in many situations. There comes a point to which it must begin to heal its pains and traumas to make room for newer experiences; good, bad, ugly, and indifferent. This is where many of our Spirits are currently at, here on this plane. In order to evolve, we will eventually play every role so we can understand all there is to this deeper knowledge of life. We will incarnate, becoming many different things, carbon-based, and otherwise, but there is always experience and purpose. Now that we are here on this plane, we have many opportunities to allow this evolution to proceed and take shape, as we need to be more than what we ever were through time and space. This is why it's necessary to heal emotionally in order to garner this deeper knowledge and wisdom of our purposes. It's above my paygrade to know what the endgame is we are inching toward. But I'll make damn sure, whatever it is, I'm going to be the best I can become, when that day comes, as we all should be.

# No More Self-Sacrificing

We can't sacrifice ourselves for convenience if we truly desire to become our authentic selves, especially if that convenience is all about someone else. In truth, we wind up compromising our own integrity and stall our own efforts to evolve. This is exactly what we've done in the past that has placed us where we currently are, and are desperately trying to come out of. This is a self-defeating pattern of people-pleasing taught to us as children, making ourselves small for the sake of someone else. We are all meant to live our lives as we see fit. This is Divine Sovereignty and one of our birthrights. We live our lives for us, not bowing to the needs of another. Indeed, we should always keep others in mind but when it comes down to it, it's our life. We can't be blatantly selfish to the point of damaging others, but we also can't be so willing to give up what is rightfully ours. This is one of the fine lines we walk on our journey, and we are the ones who decide what is right for us. We can be noble and just, at the same time, but we can't allow self-injury. In the end, we'll never know if we did what was right until we read our own Akashic Record, and our own reckoning of what was: this life.

# There Is Magic In The Unknown

How do you respond or react to change? Does it bring anxiety, dread, relief, or perhaps you tend to feel overwhelmed? Changes within our journey can bring a long-awaited transition out of our current state of being when we allow it. Change is the only constant within our lives, as we're not who we were yesterday or even minutes ago. When we embrace change, we are giving ourselves the opportunity to expand, to learn, heal, and grow. We afford ourselves hope that finally, we can overcome our current struggles. Many of us fear change, as we have been so locked into the comfort zone created many years ago and are afraid to step out of what is familiar. There is no growth, no learning, not much healing, and almost no evolution when we're stuck living in that shell. It's not us anymore. We're not the same person now, so the need to remain in our comfort zone becomes our block. We fear what we don't understand. Yet, there is magic in the unknown if you allow yourself to feel it.

## Let Your Healing Be Organic

Difficulty finding our inner peace is a telltale sign of something we need to find within, and pay close attention to. Often, it indicates that a deeper emotional healing is necessary. But what could it be and how do we find it? As with any emotional upheaval or outbreak, we must allow it to exist and honor it. It has purpose in what we feel. Honoring it means we allow it to come to the surface and let it present itself. All too often, we try to find it, which turns into an exercise in futility, and we only end up blocking the root cause. Like the energy flowing through us, simply clear your mind. Don't try to force it to manifest. Trying to force it is the block. It's a process and takes time, so don't expect it to magically appear by our search within. We don't need to become this masked emotional pain. Allow it to surface, as it will when you're ready to heal it. We can't force life, energy, or emotional healing. It has to progress organically. Go on with your day as normal, and when it's ready to come forward it will. Not until. When the answer has arrived, the healing process can begin.

## Seeing Truth When The Timing Is Right

How many times have we asked why we couldn't see the answers we've been looking for sooner than we did? Well, we weren't ready to see the truth. We had healing to do, self-discoveries to make, and a mindset to make clearer. We can't hear a message we're not ready to receive. Plain and simple. It wasn't meant to be until that ah-ha moment gently came in and kissed new life into us. Don't speak harshly to the cellular self for not knowing any better until that moment. This is a self-defeating pattern we all carry. Change it up and give yourself a lot of credit for allowing the truth to be revealed. The cellular self takes what we say as absolute truth, so we need to be cautious with even our thoughts. Change your perception to one of reward for stepping out of your current mindset, and give gratitude to yourself and your guides. Feel good about being able to rise above what was. Self-love and respect will get us farther than negative words of shame and guilt. We really don't need more of those. We are deserving of our own approval.

## The Value Of Being In The Moment

Where do you believe you need to be on your journey today? Do you wish or want to be somewhere other than where you're at? I'm not referring to your physical location, rather your spiritual outlook. Are you struggling, or are you finding ways to overcome challenges? One reminder I constantly tell my cellular self is that we're always exactly where we're meant to be. Many of us struggle within our journey because we believe our life should be different. Oftentimes, we lose sight as we lose patience with our current situation. One thought that always brings me back is to remember to be in the moment. Anxiety often means that we are living in the future, and at other times we're locked in the past, not knowing how to overcome our experience. Being in the moment allows us to be present within our mindset, and able to better handle our extremes. Being in the moment centers us within a heart-based existence where our Spirit can take over, and allow us to breathe. This is a reflection on the need to trust, and know that we're okay and we're going to be okay. If you need to hear this, then keep saying it to yourself with all the love you have.

# Blaming The Divine

When we place our trust, belief, and faith in ourselves, we are putting those in the loving hands of God, Source, however we name them. We are sovereign Divine Beings. How we treat the self, we treat the Divine. Our Spirit self is our connection to that Divine Being, so it follows that we should, with awareness, give to the self the same as we give to the Divine. I personally am guilty of misplaced emotions regarding how I see Our Father and Mother at times. It is human nature to place blame when life doesn't happen according to our expectations. I am a work in progress, and I will, at times, fall into this ego trap as it cries out its pains. When we have this realization, the next move is to center the self back into the heart space and allow the Spirit to guide us. We achieve this by letting go of expectations and attachments as to how we believe our life should be. Allow it to be organic, as it's meant to be. Choose to live from the heart, always and in all ways.

## Trust Is All We Have

During hard times, when it seems our world is crashing down around us, we are left with nothing to hold onto but trust. Hold onto that trust for dear life. Hold it close because that may be all we have. It also may be the very thing that will allow us to continue, even in our depleted state. I know how trust brought me back from the most devastating times in my life, where I faced unsurmountable odds. It was trust that allowed me to face the fact that I was told I would probably die. It was trust in myself and the Divine that has brought me here, today, 30 years after that statement from the doctor. It is that trust that allows me to know that I can and will overcome anything life throws at me. Trust is all I have had to rely on many times over, and my belief in myself and the Divine will ensure that I will continue to reign over the darkness that tries to envelope me. This is faith in something we can't see, but we know how absolutely necessary it is to never lose sight of it. It has brought me enough hope to allow me to keep living from the heart, pouring forth love to myself when I'm on my knees begging for mercy and grace. We all have this within us. Dig deep and find your faith, your trust, and your hope, for without these, who are we really? Always and in all ways, trust and believe in yourself.

# Facing Ourselves

As times become more intense, you must learn to face yourself and take care of your emotions in a healthy way. Get to know yourself at the deepest levels and befriend your darkness, allowing your own evolution. Pushing things down and living over top of your pain is a self-destructive pattern that you learned growing up from wounded people. If you don't find a way to be there for yourself and work through your emotions with self-love and gentleness, you will inevitably act out and cause harm. When intense emotions arise, like anger, sadness, and loss, be a loving parent to yourself. Find a safe space and allow your inner child and wounded ego to express their emotional state to you. Listen to what is going on deep within you, and listen with complete acceptance and healthy boundaries. Breathe love into your pain. Cry hard if you need to. But do not close down again. Allow healthy expression of what you couldn't face before. Getting to know yourself at the very deepest levels is part of self-mastery and learning to live authentically from the heart. Learn to know yourself on a much deeper level, but now add trust, belief in yourself, and an abundance of self-love.

## Keeping Our Past Out Of The Present

The awakening journey always begins with the realization that we are not who we truly are. From there it becomes a journey of unbecoming all that we are not. That journey unfolds into becoming who we are now, and not our former selves. We strive to be that which we know ourselves to be. Game on. Our soul need, and perhaps sole need, is to be free from all the limitations, projections, and pains and traumas of our former selves. This quest for freedom will last the rest of this lifetime, and probably into the next few lives when we incarnate with a new form. Indeed, the Spirit carries every memory we have ever had, and every experience we have endured, from every lifetime we have ever lived. This is why I speak so frequently of the need to heal our emotional body. We can't allow the past to remind us of who we are not now, nor who we will never be again. I have worked endlessly to keep my past out of the present, while realizing, the only way for that to come to fruition, is to allow it all to be healed to the best of my ability today. I give an enormous amount of gratitude for all of my former selves, with forgiveness. They have shaped me into who I have been, and will become. Credit given where credit is due.

## Seeing Truth

How can we say and believe that we know truth if we can't step outside of our own perception? What we choose to call truth at this point is a limited belief. Knowing truth is to allow ourselves to go beyond our knowledge, expanding our own wisdom, and accepting that there is more to ourselves than what we have experienced. Wisdom is knowing how to use knowledge, not just our own but that of our Spirit and ancestors, and being open to what is beyond our own perception. We cannot possibly see the bigger picture of our lives if we wear blinders that do not allow us to see the whole, as we do not have peripheral vision. Step outside of your perception, allow the big picture of life to show itself and see it as it is, not as you choose to see it. Seeing truth is seeing outside of our perspective and our limited experiences.

## Self-Care During Difficult Times

As we find ourselves on a fast-track to our personal evolution, our lives may get disrupted, and we are shaken out of our comfort zone. These are not easy times for our nervous system, which usually requires a slow steady pace of familiarity. Most of us feel quite overwhelmed these days, with the daily increase in chaos and violence in our outer world. We may notice how deeply we are connected with all of humanity via the Collective Consciousness.

The frequency of Mother Earth is steadily increasing, as it must in her ascension process, and we are basically hanging on for dear life, trying to keep up with the energetic changes and what arise in our personal lives. We are confronted with our own darkness, our fears, rage, victim mentality, and unprocessed traumas. Our mental and emotional patterns, passed down from the generations before us, are in our face. It is, at times, very tempting to slip back into the blame game and project our unwanted emotions onto those around us.

We have to work overtime to keep up with what comes up to be healed, while trying to maintain a sense of integrity and sanity. For many of us, our sleep patterns are disrupted, and when the world around us is finally quiet, we lie awake, processing and healing.

Some of us experience a profound loneliness during these times, as those who previously made up our circle are also quite busy with themselves. For many of us, people close to us are dropping out of our lives, as the previous resonance is not there anymore. This is the Universe clearing what no longer serves our highest good out of our lives. Sometimes, we simply have evolved and changed in such a way that others cannot follow us where we are going. It is so important to trust ourselves, our journey, and the Divine, and allow the necessary changes in our lives.

Please know that we are all struggling, in one form or another, as we live through these times of great upheaval and intensity. Find the simplicity in your life again. Do the dishes when everything is swirling around you. Make yourself a cup of tea. Go for a walk. Try to see beauty in your life again. We are learning to be our own best friend and give ourselves the love and support that we need. This is also a part of our personal evolution.

This world needs us right now, more than ever. Those who can face themselves and their own darkness, healing our self-defeating patterns, and emerging stronger under the tutelage of our own self-love, are the bringers of the New. This doesn't mean that we are not deeply struggling with the crumbling of the old structures and systems, within and without. We are birthing the new world as we build a new foundation within us, for living from the heart.

## The Gift Of Trust

Everything is different with trust. When we are able to surrender our need for control and our fears, at the deepest level, to the Divine, we are able to allow what is, and embrace our natural vulnerability. In this raw state of openness, we are able to see from a higher perspective and find safety in our connectedness. We realize how much we are loved and cared for by the Divine. How much we are being guided, carried, and nurtured through the ups and downs of our earthly existence. We can embrace change with trust and calm our fears, knowing that we will be okay no matter what happens in our lives because we are completely supported by the Universe. We can allow this messy earthly journey to be what it is meant to be, as we are learning our soul lessons one day at a time, without constantly interjecting our need to have things a certain way. With trust, we can let go of the stifling limitations of our comfort zone, and venture out into the uncharted open spaces where magic happens, and where we are able to experience our freedom.

## Healing Our Ancestral Lineage

We all grew up with projections from our family, some more damaging than others. We can no longer place blame on them for our actions now. In essence, we are saying that they are responsible for our actions, making them accountable for what we do. We deny our own accountability for what comes from us. Their past projections can no longer be used as justification for choosing to not own our actions. As adults we have a responsibility to heal the woundedness within us that their manipulations brought. Yes, ancestral traits are very real, but healing them within us, now, is the only way to break the mold and heal the ancestral line, ending the continuation of toxic projections. More important than any of the traits we inherit, is our responsibility to effectively eradicate those traits within ourselves to the best of our ability, and being accountability for our actions. This will clear the karmic debt left for us to heal by our ancestors.

# Transitional Phases On Our Journey

As we reach the ending of another phase on our journey, there are many changes within. We allow what no longer serves us to be replaced, making space for what will serve us in this new phase. This transitional phase can bring much confusion, and in some cases, we find that we need to mourn the loss of what we became comfortable within. We must keep up with the inner changes taking place. We need to find our new frequency, and we must implement many new beliefs and patterns. I have found that changing up the old routines to fit within the new serves me well. This breaks us from the confinements and limitations we unknowingly set. Ahh... freedom... As we reinvent ourselves to settle into a new phase, we find unincumbered freedom since we have everywhere to go. We find expansion within, as we grow and evolve from our yesterday. Be gentle and nurturing with the self as we navigate so much newness. Now is our time as a co-creator to build a stronger foundation for our future self.

# Phoenix Out Of The Ashes

Grief hurts, trauma hurts, being yanked out of everything we have known hurts. And yet in our open state of woundedness, our healing ability is also increased. On an emotional level we heal not only from the soul crushing thing that just happened, but we also heal much of our past traumas as we go through the motions and stages of healing. And slowly, with time, we move on, dust ourselves off and after long phases in the dark, we begin to crawl back out and seek the light. Little by little, we find our will again, our drive, and our excitement for life. Yet, we are new, and like a baby learning to walk. We are wobbly on the legs, a little timid, and weary of the world but we walk forward, nonetheless. Our head still held low for a while. We gain momentum, and the hope that runs through our veins activates, and carries us forward to a new and fresh life. What we experienced... the trauma, the rupture, the abyss of pain, is no small death. A part of us died when we could not tolerate our experience, only for it to become the compost from which our new life is springing. Phoenix out of the ashes, rising in a quantum leap. The resurrection of cell and psyche. A full circle of life and death, and back to life again. What is a miracle if not this? The miracle of life itself, within each of us.

## We Are Not Who We Have Become

Deep down and underneath it all, we believe that we are our darkness. The toxic family patterns that have been projected onto us have been passed down from generation to generation, and are coursing through our veins still, reminding us of pain and trauma. Our survival mechanisms are tangible in all aspects of our existence, and our controlling nature has become the fabric of our lives. Our soul crushing experiences have molded us into someone other than our authentic self. And we identify with the assemblage of survival mechanisms we believe is our self, and hate ourselves for it. This, however, is not who we are. It is what was projected onto us, which we have adopted as ourselves. Yet, underneath the darkness we identify with lies the precious, innocent self that we have forgotten. That is who we are in essence. Everything lying heavy and dark over top of it was added, usually against our will. But own it, we must - not what was done to us, but who we have become through it all. We are adults, now, and have run out of blame. The darkness is a part of us now, and so we must heal it, but not become it and not identify with it. Allow the process of changing these dissonant patterns and heal your woundedness. That is your responsibility. On the other side awaits the discovery of your innermost being, your Divine Spirit, residing in your heart space.

## Learning Grace

We have to honor the Divine sovereignty of those we love. We cannot save them from their soul contracts that have been written before they were born. We cannot persuade them to do things our way, even if it were healthier for them, as their journey has to unfold according to their nature, not ours. We do not know what experiences they need to have in this lifetime. And while we may have an urgent desire to help and to protect them, it is not our place to stifle their freedom or authenticity in any way. We are learning grace - to love and support, and hold space but not control others. This is the undoing of our codependence. We are stepping into our own freedom, and learning to let our relationships be based on freedom, as well. To love without attachment and yet open our hearts wide.

# Honesty About Our Own Toxic Behaviors

All of us carry toxic traits within us that affect our lives, whether we are aware of them, or not. Most of these destructive patterns are trauma and survival responses that were passed down from the generations before us, and are deeply engrained in our cellular self and emotional body. We have become good at hiding the darkness that lies beneath the surface, even from ourselves. Yet, when we get triggered, our woundedness usually pushes its way forward, overtaking our speech and interactions. In conflict situations we may get called out by others about these toxic, hurtful behaviors that seem to have a life of their own, at times pushing our normal composure and inner boundaries aside, and wreaking havoc.

When awareness of our dysfunctional character traits is being brought to us, we are wise to listen. It will be harder to discern what is truth when the words are mixed with anger and projections. But when we have a quiet moment to ourselves, we may discover that we have actually been presented with something important about ourselves. It is a gift to have a newfound awareness of our own destructiveness and how we sabotage our lives, as much as our wounded ego dislikes that kind of honesty. We are wise to take a deeper look and see how our own unconscious darkness is hurting ourselves and others.

With awareness, we have choice, and choice is the bridge to our personal freedom. With discernment, we can pick out the pearls among the words of another person and use them to find a deeper honesty with ourselves. While we may deeply dislike what has been brought to light about us, we must remember that we are not our behaviors. How we act is learned, starting in early childhood, but who we are is not really connected to our own toxic survival patterns or conditioning. Who we are is the essence of our self.

Keeping this in mind may make it easier to roll up our sleeves and get to work on the self-defeating or hurtful patterns that we display in our interactions with others and ourselves. As such, we are learning to allow constructive criticism, accept other people's boundaries, and be receptive to an honest response to our own dysfunction, when it comes from a trusted source.

Without honesty, we cannot heal. It is certainly not anyone's job to point out our flaws, and they should not be permitted to make a habit of it, or say things to tear us down. But many of us are nowadays in relationships that are centered on mutual respect and support of our healing journeys. It maybe be difficult, at first, to set our woundedness aside and not rush into trigger mode, when we are presented with a piece of truth about our own toxic behaviors. Instead of deflecting the new awareness that is being brought to us, we can use it to further our own healing. We can be open and say, "Show me what I am doing that is hurting you…" rather than becoming defensive.

We all carry violence in our cells and darkness in our hearts, and we don't actually mean to project this onto our loved ones, tearing them down. We are learning to face ourselves with courage and to be accountable for all that comes from the self, including what is yet hidden from our awareness. We have to deeply trust ourselves on this. With a bit of practice, we will no longer let constructive criticism throw us into a destructive self-pity or victim mode, but actually own, head held high, what is ours and do the inner work that we came here to do.

Please remember that we are all human, and as such damaged in our relationship with ourselves and others, and in our psychological and emotional landscape. Our ancestors are cheering us on, supporting our every attempt at overcoming what they could not, and all the inner work we do to build a better world through our own healing.

# The Purposes Of Our Incarnation

This human being thing is hard. We're a Spirit with form, experiencing so that we can evolve. A Spirit cannot evolve without form, so here we are, a Spirit in form, experiencing. It can be such a harsh experience on Earth, but we incarnated at this time because we can heal much faster here. It is by no means easier, just faster. The dense atmosphere on our planet creates the ability to go deeper, with an accelerated pace. It is more intense but when we hopefully achieve our purposes, we move on to the next phase of our journey, back home. Yes, our purposes. We have a series of purposes laid out before our incarnation, intent on furthering our evolution. When one is completed, we move onto the next purpose, and that pattern continues into the next incarnation. This is a never-ending cycle because we will always have something to learn, to heal, and grow with expansion. We'll know when we read our Akashic Record, when we cross over, how well we followed our journey as it was contracted, or not. We will only be judged by our own Spirit as to our accomplishments. What will your Spirit see in your life here on Earth? What will be your legacy?

## Moving On From Our Traumas

As we heal emotionally, we have a tendency to keep revisiting our pain and trauma. We subconsciously relive it, keeping it alive within. What we are effectively doing is giving it the energy to exist. Stop giving it energy and it cannot live. We become consumed by it, as it takes over our life. The problem is not the painful experience, but our need to keep reliving it. Accepting that it happened will help us move beyond it, transforming the trauma. Since our journey is an upward spiral, we always come back to the place where it exists within our memory, giving us a chance to heal yet another layer. Every time a traumatic memory or emotion comes up, give it love, offer it forgiveness, and tell it you no longer hold space for it. I found that as the visual memory came back, I would see it shrink until it disappeared, as I told it I could no longer hold space for it. This is not denial of the pain or the experience, but a method of healing that truly worked for me, especially for the ones hardest to heal. As with any emotional healing, it will in time cease to exist, if we do the inner work. When we are no longer triggered, we can begin to consider it healed, and finally say goodbye, moving onto the next one.

# The Process of Internal Checks And Balances

Regardless of what type of journey you're on, keeping yourself in check daily, even constantly, is always a good idea. Questioning your actions and your motivations will keep you honest and on your path. Ask yourself, "Why did I do this in that manner? What was my motive in deciding my actions?" as you reflect upon your day. Become the observer and step outside of your perception to see the truth. Being the observer, and seeing from the Spirit self, allows us to see truth from a higher perspective, not the ego self. This self-reflection is, in part, self-mastery. It helps us change the harmful patterns and beliefs of the old self, replacing them with the new that is meant for our highest good. This system of checks and balances has been in use since mankind formed its first government millennia ago, and has been a proven system. The right hand must always know what the left hand is doing, and vice versa. This brings a balancing insight into who we truly are, and helps us learn what changes we need to make within ourselves to become our authentic self.

# Rising Beyond our Yesterdays

Realization of a truth higher than our knowledge is a natural flow of evolution. There will always be new truth, knowledge, and wisdom beyond our every today. Allowing ourselves to receive all that is meant for us on a Spirit level will ensure that we transcend our every yesterday, in all aspects of our lives. Freedom occurs when we begin to unbecome who we have been taught to be, realizing our true authenticity. We are given many opportunities to learn, grow, and heal. As long as we stay away from being a victim to the necessary changes being made, we will certainly rise above our challenges. Allowance to change can and will facilitate change. Don't allow the fear of leaving the box that we've existed within to override the natural progressions of evolution. There is, indeed, magic within the unknown.

# Our Loved Ones In The Etheric

When the tragic loss of a loved one comes into our lives and our hearts, the pain can be devastating. It is indeed the most painful loss we can endure. Allow the grieving process to be as you need it to be, with patience and compassion for yourself. One thing that we must understand is that separation is an illusion. We are all connected in the Etheric through a common thread. No, they are no longer here in their 3D presence, but look around you. They are in everything we see. Hugs may not be possible, but they are with us regardless. We choose to either exist within the pain of our loss, or we choose to embrace the gifts they brought us. Their smile, their laugh, the life they brought to us, the way they could touch people, and see beauty. Keep them alive in our hearts and they will never leave our side. Life is not necessarily easier with time, but we can find peace within the changes we become. We may have lost much in the 3D, but I choose to believe we have gained a guide, always present, always watching over us, until it is our time to meet again. That is such a powerful healing: to know they take care of us, even in their physical absence.

## Facing Our Own Mortality

Physical death is an unfortunate reality in our evolution. Some of us will be blessed to live long productive lives, and some will have a short-lived existence here. How you face death will depend on how you perceive it, and how you lived your life. Will you see regrets and missed opportunities, or will you embrace it, knowing you lived your life to its fullest, and did the very best you could with what you had. We cannot wait until the end, only to see where we could have changed what we needed to. So, we must do what is necessary as life happens, making the necessary changes through the opportunities the Universe brings us. Ask yourself, what will be my legacy? What will I leave behind that made a difference, not only for myself but for the world? Did I do all I could, or did I do just enough to just get by, barely surviving? We always have a choice in how we respond to the experiences that life brings us, and we always have the opportunity to change our lives at any time. Look back on your life while you are still able and make the changes you need to make. Live your life to its fullest and truly be alive while you're here. Perhaps it is better to regret something we did than something we should have done because you may never have another chance.

# Experiencing and Feeling Deeply

Why must we feel pain to the depths that we do? This question has plagued me for many years. The loss we feel is because as a Spirit on a healing journey, we must feel all the extremes to their fullest. This is how the Spirit learns, heals, and grows. Our contracts for this incarnation determine our experiences but we determine the depths to which we feel. The more open we are, living from the heart, the more painful or intense our feelings. This too, shall pass, as all eventually does. We have been forever changed, with a clearer understanding, and the ability to heal on a much deeper level. It's all about opening the 3D self to the heart space, where the Spirit resides, to experience all we can on an even deeper level than before. We are not being punished; this is our evolution.

## The Pitfalls Of Channeling And Psychic Readings

Many of us are on a journey of reconnecting with the higher dimensions, communing with our own Spirit, and talking with our spirit guides, angels, ascended masters, and Mother/Father God. This is a part of opening our awareness and third eye, accessing our intuitive gifts, and strengthening our clairvoyance, clairaudience, and clairsentience. There is nothing more valuable and helpful in our lives than a direct communication that gives us true guidance.

But there are many pitfalls to this, as well. Because we are hearing these voices in our own heads, we must always question if we are actually hearing information from the Divine. The message we believe we are hearing may originate from a wounded part of ourselves that doesn't want to give up control, and is trying to give us the information we want to hear. And if we are certain that the information is not coming from our ego, is it actually coming from the source that we think it is? Use discernment, always.

If you are channeling or doing psychic readings, or believe you are getting information from a certain higher being, ask them if they are from the light, and to identify themselves. Have them show you their energy signature and feel into their energy. If you are given specific information about the future, that is likely a red flag, as we are rarely meant to know what is coming in the future. I have personally had intergalactic teenagers play pranks on me, as well as catching my wounded ego trying to push an agenda by posing as the voice of the Divine. Disconnect and break communication immediately if your gut feeling says that the voice is not who they claim to be. Use your intuition.

There is so much false information out there right now, with many claiming to channel the highest beings and truths, when their agenda, coming from their woundedness, is really to finally feel important, and thrive in the spiritual marketplace. Many folks offering psychic readings are also unaware as to the source of their information, and that they can only see an image in time, which may be a future possibility, but is never an absolute truth, as there are too many variables to provide specifics.

We must learn to discern as our minds are opening and we are exploring the higher realms, whether through our own connection or through someone channeling or giving psychic readings. Deceiving ourselves or letting ourselves be deceived by someone claiming to have the highest answers for us only adds an unnecessary detour to our journey. You are deserving of true connection with the higher dimensions. This is why it is essential to trust yourself and your intuition - with discernment always.

## Creating New Reference Points

We are creating a new reference point for every experience we are gifted. We have added to the Collective as well as our own journey for future use. Eventually, we will come across a similar experience with much different variables. Although we cannot use the same exact wisdom within this new event as an outcome, we have gained knowledge that is useful now. We have a way to gauge our response accordingly, and are better equipped in resolving a new issue. This is evolution. We have a new awareness, with a broader scope, and recognition from seeing more of the bigger picture. With the wisdom we now have, we can better use our knowledge to not only see truth quicker but save ourselves needless struggles. We can find a better way through trust and belief in ourselves to allow a deeper healing that will follow the experience. We have a better understanding of how to heal yet another layer that has come forward to be healed, taking it to an even deeper level. This is the process of emotional healing at work, going within, doing what we need to ensure our evolution toward the authentic self. The unbecoming of who and what we never were.

# The Process Of Changing Our Mindset

We have all been programmed to believe that change, healing, and even receiving what we want has to be an immediate event. It's not. It's a process. Changing that belief begins with allowing it to be a process. It's a mindset. Patience. Those are hard lessons to learn but if we don't learn them, they will remain huge blocks on our journey and in our personal lives. To change these beliefs and patterns, we need to stop our thought process, and learn to say no. Enough. Choose to allow the mindset change from the old and implement the new. You have the awareness, now follow through with the recognition of the old. Replace it with the new. It's not an event. It's a process that we must allow, with patience and diligence. It's always the right time to end the madness we've been living, and allow freedom in every aspect of our lives.

## Feeling Our Emotions Fully

You may feel irritated and anxious, as many of us do these days, while we individually and collectively move through this turbulent phase of transition to a higher frequency and level of consciousness. Do not turn away from your discomfort and emotional pain, and distract yourself, but invite it in. Allow yourself to fully feel whatever presents itself, and breathe. Hold yourself and give yourself acceptance. Make time to follow the thread all the way down to the origin of the agony. Be the observer and allow awareness to come. Lift it into your heart and pour love and compassion into it. As you do this, you will notice a change. You are not resisting your pain and discomfort anymore. You are not trying to run or hide from it, and you are no longer in victim mode. By giving it your full attention, you are able to feel, heal, release, and then move on, with patience as to the time that this process takes. Regardless of what may be going on, you have found YOU again, and you are no longer lost – as you believed you were before in your perception. You may not know what is going on, but that is not necessary. You are again able to trust that you are exactly where you need to be.

# Balance And The Aquarian Age

The patriarchal system is crumbling as we are transitioning into the age of Aquarius, the time of the Sacred Feminine. This is a time of balance for all genders, not bringing more division, one gender against the other, highlighting duality and exclusion. The unhealed, toxic feminine is just as damaging as the toxic, dominating masculine. Women are not all goddesses and men are not all perpetrators. The common need is for all of us to heal our traumatic childhoods, as we grew up with deeply wounded people who projected their rage and emotional issues onto us, putting us down when we needed their love. This is an import time in history, with women and men finding their innate power and connection to the Divine within, and learning to live from the heart. There is absolutely no need to continue the terrible power games of superiority, abuse, and exploitation. Going within the self and connecting with our Divine Spirit, we all have limitless energy, strength, love, and wisdom at our disposal, not needing to be takers. It is time to accept that control, superiority, and inferiority are illusions, and to allow our own evolution, breaking those damaging patterns and being accountable. It is time to empower the peaceful authenticity of all who share this planet.

## Making Your Stand

We all have a role to play within the universal shift currently taking place, and there are purposes beyond our understanding. There are also common grounds on which we all must make our contribution. We all must anchor the Light to Gaia, building a strong foundation for the New Day and New Way, as promised to us. It is also imperative for us all to put an end to feeding the strong masculine ego that needs to control by means of fear. We can no longer enable those who would control and manipulate those they deem weak and unworthy of existence. There is a need for us all to set healthy boundaries to protect ourselves from the very predators who would like to take our freedom, and continue to desire to dominate those who bring change. Make your stand and protect that which is sacred in Spirit - our energy, our hearts, and our birthrights as limitless Beings.

# Our Divine Heritage

The Divine, God, Source, needs no human definition. We cannot grasp what and who this consciousness really is that created us, along every molecule of this Universe, and how It thinks and operates. We all have the connection, as our Spirit is of the Divine, child to the All. To me personally, from my visions and communications, there is the Divine Mother consciousness that is the creator of all that is. She is love. She is essence and nurturer. She is symbiotically connected to all her children. The Divine Father, as much a part of Her as She is of Him - in complete Oneness - is the activator, truth bringer, and CEO of the whole universal operation. It is He who holds the plan for this current shift on Earth. It is He who guides us, personally, on our journey, often through our spirit guides, guardians, and angels, who are in service to Father/Mother, the Holy One. We share in their power, their life, and their love. Never separate, our Spirit is an inherent part of the Divine in an ever-expanding dance of creation and evolution.

# The Dangers of the Bliss Bunny Syndrome

To truly be able to heal, we must be willing to face reality as it is, not as we imagine it to be. As we are able to allow truth and honesty to expand within us, we are able to take off the rosy glasses through which we have tried to deal with our wounds and our lives. For many of us, the mental and emotional dissociation started at a young age when we were traumatized. From our early developmental stage at the time, we created illusions that we could feel comfortable and safe within, as part of our survival mechanisms, since our reality was often unbearable to us.

And many of us have used spiritual ideals in our adult lives to continue living in a fantasy world of our own making, as we simply have never found our way back to living in reality. Things are distorted in this place of make-believe. Neither discernment nor healthy boundaries exist here to keep us safe. We simply manipulate our perception to match the outcome we want, and voila, we are happy, and everything seems to be going our way.

And yet we have completely lost any true gauge of reality, of other people's intentions, and of our own intuition and higher guidance. We have become the determiners of what is real and what isn't. With little ability to make wise decisions, we cannot assess facts. We believe, like a child, that what we "see" is all there is. And since we first mentally create what we want see, affirming our fantasies, we feel that we have proof that our perceptions are, indeed, factual reality.

This is a dangerous game, and many "bliss bunnies" have fallen into the hands of ever-so-charming narcissists, wo exploited them for everything they had, leaving them feeling even more broken. Yet, these con people, who in their own way know how to manipulate reality to their liking, have also provided a wakeup call for those hopelessly mired in their own rosy bubble. Our relationships with narcissists have devastated us to our core and to a point where we couldn't put our illusions back together. They ripped open our dissociative mental defenses and left us having to face the shattered reality of our lives.

Many of us find ourselves these days learning discernment in a hurry, trying to implement healthy, protective boundaries so that we don't fall prey to the lies of these exploiters ever again. We are trying to undo a lifetime of bad decisions and face ourselves, for maybe the first time in our lives. It takes time to shift our inner environment to feeling safe within ourselves, eyes wide open, and deal with life on life's terms. But we are learning, healing, and growing as we sit within the reality of our lives, without numbing ourselves via some illusionary manipulation of our perception. We are learning to accept reality as it is and find our power in how we act and react. We don't have to be in control of everything anymore. Life, as it really is, is enough - one moment at a time.

# The Importance Of Internal Boundaries

When we come to a point within our healing process where anger and rage take over our emotions, grace is buried beneath our pain. We tend to lash out at those undeserving who care about us. I was told as a child repeatedly, "If you can't say anything nice, then keep your mouth shut." What a perfect time to put this to use, when we have lost ourselves deep within our anguish. Isolate, find a safe haven to rage, if you need to, but don't project your raw emotions onto others. They aren't deserving of receiving your pain. You'll only end up saying hurtful words that can't be taken back, tearing another down. You've just created an unsafe environment for them, and it can only get ugly from there. This is why we must have internal and external boundaries. Restrain your emotions before you cause irreparable damage to those around you. Find your grace, keep your dignity and that of others, and you won't push them away. Abide by your own healthy internal boundaries that are meant to keep you from overstepping the boundaries of those around you.

# Finding The Strength To Go On

We're allowed to feel run-down, tired, frazzled, exhausted, and on our last leg. Emotional healing takes much energy, and sometimes it feels as if we have no more to give. Take today and allow that to exist, for tomorrow you're going to find something within you that you may not have recognized. Suddenly, we find the strength, courage, and grace to continue in the same fashion as yesterday. And when we finally call it a day, we can say, "I did it! I lived another day!" My hat comes off for every one of you. Each day that we awaken from our nightly reprieve we came out on top of yesterday. Be proud of yourself. Treat yourself to something special. Don't stand on your laurels, though, because more healing is coming, but take the time to recognize every triumph and victory you've earned. You've come a long way since you became aware of this journey. Kudos to you, with my admiration. Always remember that all is temporary. Don't give up. Don't ever give up.

## Allowing Our Relationships To Change

Most of us feel quite alone in this life and long for others to share our journey with, whether they are in the form of a partner, best friends, or a community. When we have needs, our minds often try to fit what we find in our external world to our desires, creating an illusion about the person rather than seeing the whole picture. We may believe someone to be our best friend without ever truly knowing them.

We are wise to remember that people usually show us the side of themselves that they want us to see, hiding the dysfunction that may have us reject them. We can go on for decades not really knowing folks in our close circle, believing they are all kinds of wonderful, when we only see them occasionally and on their best, long-rehearsed behavior. This may be especially the case if the other wants our approval or looks up to us in any way. We must always be open to learning more about the people in our lives, and believe them when they show us who they truly are.

As we are evolving and becoming truer to our own nature, learning discernment and healthy boundaries, we need to also allow increased awareness in all aspects of our lives. Becoming the observer, we are suddenly able to see aspects of others that had escaped us while our perception was limited by our own needs and wounds. This doesn't mean that we now go looking for faults or toxic traits in others, but that we stay true to ourselves and allow our relationships to change.

Since we are all evolving, and often in different directions, there is no status quo to hold onto. The more we are able to feel grounded and secure in our relationship with ourselves, the more we can let others be who they are, without making it about us. We no longer have to change them or carry their burdens. We are much better able to stand on our own feet, while being able to give and receive love and support, without the codependence that would distort our interactions.

Allowing our relationships to evolve and change, as they naturally do, gives us the opportunity to practice non-attachment. This provides an opening to those around us and ourselves, freeing all of us to be authentic, with accountability and honesty. And if the resonance is no longer there with a person, then it will be much easier for us to go with the flow and wish them well from the heart. We are not taking it personal that we have evolved in different ways, and our paths are no longer shared in the way that they were.

Not all relationships are meant to last a lifetime. Many are much shorter encounters where valuable gifts and lessons are exchanged, as it was contracted before we incarnated, and then we go on with our lives, hopefully in gratitude for what we received.

# There Can Be No Evolution Without Trust

One of the hardest lessons we will ever learn is to lay down our armor, shield, and swords. There is no longer anything to fight for, as we learn to live from the heart in every aspect of our lives. I know the raw vulnerability that we must embrace during this transition, but I also know how it feels to be on the other side of not allowing our trust. Indeed… we must learn to trust. When we trust ourselves, our journey, the process, and God, we can surrender believing we are in control. Allow what is meant to be to flow to you and through you with ease, in every aspect of your life. I've used this mantra for years, and knowing we're not in control frees up that energy to focus on our journey. Honestly, it takes less energy to not try and control our lives than it does trying to control it. Put that energy to better use evolving. There can be no evolution without trust.

# Trusting The Processes Of Healing

After every round of healing that we finish, is a transition. This means we must find our frequency again, and we are incredibly raw and vulnerable. Now is the time to release what has been healed and what you are still healing. Exhale and allow it to flow outward. Often, when we can't feel our energy, we feel lost and very unsure. This is natural and a part of the healing process. Not knowing where we belong, we tend to accentuate what we don't understand causing unnecessary confusion. This is where trust comes into play. We will not hit the hard stop when we trust, as the Divine will not allow us to. Without trust there is no evolution. Each transition is our evolution. All the hard work we have put into healing does, indeed, pay off in the end. Visit yourself a year ago, ten years, even twenty years ago, if you're old enough, and see how far you've come. Don't stay long. Just long enough to see you then. This is your evolution, and you should celebrate, just don't settle on your laurels. Job well done, y'all.

## The Balance Of Dark And Light

Balance in every aspect of our lives is a necessity on our journey. Life is not all light and love, as spirituality may have us believe, nor is it shining our light so brightly that it takes the darkness away. There is meaning behind the yin-yang symbol that shows the necessity to balance dark and light, for they exist in balance, with and within each other. To understand this concept means we accept our darkness within, for if we deny any part of our self, we deny our whole self and only accept what we perceive to be good. Believing we can exist in a constant state of bliss is to deny all within us that needs to be healed. We continue to push it all down, robbing ourselves of necessary experiences for our evolution. It is the wounded ego trying to control our very existence, and in truth, we are sabotaging our journey and our evolution by not accepting ourselves as we are. We cannot be authentic until we have total acceptance and love for ourselves, good and bad, in equal measure. The energy we use to deceive ourselves is the same energy we use to do the inner work that we came here to accomplish. As we do this inner work, we will find that through healing emotionally we bring healing to our wounded ego, and create the balance we need in our lives.

# Believing In Yourself Again

To trust and believe in yourself means that you know your worth, trust your intuition, respect, and honor yourself, and have forgiven yourself thoroughly. It means that you have found self-acceptance. With this as your goal, you will encounter much that needs to be healed within, and layers upon layers of conditioning to be shed. So, do it and dig down all the way to the faulty cornerstones of your previous life, built by being a pawn in someone else's game. Let it all be washed away by the healing waters of your tears. Release all that has been trapped inside. Make no excuses. Excavate what crushed your soul, feel it deeply, and release it with love. Who you thought you were, was a mistaken perception – that is all. It is now time to move on. Gather your broken pieces, and put all your passion, will, and love into putting yourself back together anew, building a new foundation for your life. Believe in yourself like your life depends on it – because it does.

# Bringing Change For Future Generations

We all feel the need to make the world a better place than it is. Unfortunately, we will not see our efforts come to fruition, but that cannot stop us from continuing what was started by the "First Wave Blue Rays" during the 1940's. Their world was in much turmoil, creating a transitional period in our history, and they saw the need to live from the heart and the need for love. This was the dawning of the Age of Aquarius, helping usher in the Divine Feminine energy. We are in that age now, and they figured out much of what we know by being aware of truths other than what they had been shown. We must continue, not for us, but for those generations to come. It is a process that takes time, and there will be no single event during this shift to a higher consciousness. We need to trust and know that we are making a difference for those growing up after us, for they will inherit what we leave behind. These are our children, grandchildren, and great-grandchildren. Teach them well. Show them how to live from the heart. Show them how to love and be love. That's how we are going to change the world. But it starts with all of us, living as an example for them to follow.

# Our Birthright Of Freedom

Stand tall in your freedom to choose how you live your life. There is no human with the right to tell us how we can and cannot live our lives. The need of the few to control the many is coming to an end as humanity evolves out of the darkness of patriarchal rule and domination. We all have free will and we must exercise those rights divinely inherent. The freedom given to us is one of our birthrights, as is our birthright to live as we choose, not as another demands. They may want to impose their beliefs. We absolutely do not have to accept their attempts to control us. Simply deny their efforts and stand up for what you believe in. Another birthright meant for us all is to believe as we do without persecution from those who believe otherwise. Choose to be authentically you. Choose to deny them any attempt to control you. Stand up for your rights as a human being, a limitless being, and a free Spirit. Choose freedom.

## The True Power Of The Enabler

If we all collectively stopped enabling the wounded ego of those around us, and worked with dedication on healing our own, the state of the world would change radically within a relatively short period of time, and be a place where we could finally all thrive, including our mistreated planet. The role of the enabler is a powerful position that gives our approval, energy, and resources to those who act out in controlling behavior, violence, and false authority. When we allow others to belittle, use, or abuse us, no matter how subtle, we are playing an active role in giving them our power. Traditionally women played the role of coddling the men in their lives from a subservient place, continually taking away the consequences of their anger-driven actions. We are now in a place where we all must learn to undo our transgenerational conditioning, and stop giving our sovereign power away to those who lay claim to it. As we are discovering our own authenticity, and working our way through our own self-defeating and codependent behaviors, we are feeling less responsible for the feeling of others, allowing them to deal with their own lives. This is truly empowering to all, including those stuck in bullying behaviors. Without our enabling behavior, they, too, finally have a chance to break the cycle that their ancestors were stuck in, learning accountability, and new and better ways of being.

# Finding Your Courage

The belief that it is best to err on the side of caution is an incredibly limiting notion. We were programmed as children to fear the possibility of what could go wrong. How will we ever know what could truly be possible if we limit ourselves to the fear of failure? Instead of accepting failure before we even begin, change your mindset to that of making possibility and success come to life. Trust and believe this: the answer will always be no if you don't try or ask. Simple enough. No one has ever become successful without taking calculated risks. Don't shut down what may have been meant for you and your journey because of some fear instilled in us as kids. Find your courage and strength to allow what could be yours by Divine inheritance, or what was always meant to be for you. Stop controlling your life and your evolution, and start asking what will go right instead of what could go wrong.

## Self-Forgiveness For What Was Done To Us

When we have experienced abuse at the hands or words of another, there is psychological damage that occurred. This is especially the case when we hold any kind of love for the perpetrator, whether they were a parent, friend, or partner to us. We don't actually hate them, deep down, for what was done to us. We hate ourselves. We disconnect from our own self and close our heart towards our own being.

It is generally much easier for us to forgive another, even for the most soul crushing brutalities, but to forgive ourselves can seem to be a near impossible task. In the process of forgiving the one who brought the violence, we can see how they passed on what was done to them in their childhood, how they projected their emotions when they could no longer find a way to handle them, or tried desperately, despite their own toxic upbringing, to be the best person they could. If there was once love in our heart for them, we can find it again, and absolve them from the anger and hate we felt towards them for the injustice that was put on us.

But to forgive ourselves and stop the self-punishment, we need to dig yet a lot deeper. Our relationship with ourselves shattered when the trauma occurred, and it can be difficult to find a way to enter this space of self-forgiveness. We usually took on the shame and blame for what was done to us, holding ourselves guilty for something that was completely outside of our own control, and acted out by another. We may feel dirty, rotten to the core, flawed, or broken, habitually rejecting and abandoning ourselves, still many years or decades after the abuse.

Many children feel that they deserved the atrocities committed against them. At their developmental level at the time, they tried to resolve their ruptured consciousness by turning the blame against themselves, and this still festers inside of ourselves as adults. We loathe ourselves without actually knowing why. It is an abstract blanket rejection of the self, rather than not liking certain unhealthy traits in ourselves for a reason.

This is where we need to dig deep and reframe our experiences, changing our engrained trauma responses and perspective. It may be important to pull our inner child close, and look realistically and honestly at what our part was in our traumatic experience. Were we in the wrong place at the wrong time? Or did we actually, from our adult perspective, do anything to provoke and deserve the attack upon our person? Are we taking accountability away from the person who is responsible for the violence against us, and instead putting it on ourselves?

When we sit, time and again, with our internal devastation, and bravely unpack and feel our emotions surrounding the event, we are creating internal movement. Soon, we will be able to find it easier to breathe, and notice that our heart is softening and slowly opening toward the self.

With the practice of compassion and self-acceptance, we can start to appreciate who we truly are, instead of rejecting ourselves unconsciously because of something bad that happened to us a long time ago. We can, in time, forgive ourselves and let go at a cellular level, creating space for a new, loving relationship with ourselves and the beautiful life we deserve.

# Learning To Receive

I remember, not long after I moved two thousand miles from where I was, a stranger told me that the reason I didn't have what I wanted the most was because I wanted it too much. He told me I was creating my own block by making it a need. It was for me the figure out how to unblock this within myself. I discovered that I had to take away the importance of it. It couldn't be controlled just because I had an expectation. In fact, my expectation was the block. My perception of its arrival, just because I wanted it and needed it, was my attempt to control life. By taking away the importance of it, I released the expectation, putting myself back in this moment, and allowing life to be as it's meant to be. I was manipulating what I believed I had control over. When I learned to change that self-defeating pattern, I found what was mine – what I contracted for before I incarnated here. My expectation was holding me back from my evolution. That was truly one of the hardest lessons for me to learn. And I don't believe I'll ever stop learning the lessons, I may have previously thought I had mastered. I'm content, knowing I'm a work in progress.

## Living In Grace

I never knew what grace meant until a tragic event forced me to find it. Years later, my journey showed me how to live in grace. To live in grace means to live from the heart, the Spirit self, with gratitude, appreciation, and humility for all that life has brought. Experiences are neutral. Our wounded ego gives them definition. Energy is neutral. Our perception and intention give it definition. Living in grace is the ability to step outside of our perception, allowing the Spirit to step forward, and seeing truth, not something we perceive from our woundedness. It is the ability to not be judgmental, rather being open to seeing from our heart, not our past experiences. Each experience is new, sometimes similar in content, but totally unrelated to every experience that has gone before. Living in grace allows us to see each experience as unique, each being unique. Living in grace is knowing inner peace and the ability to see beauty in everything.

# Doing What We Must

It's not necessary for us to constantly justify what we do, especially when it's something that must be done. We already have the mindset of not purposely bringing harm to the self and others. As long as we remain true to ourselves, there is no need to explain anything. We must allow ourselves to do as we must to ensure our evolution. There will always be a factor of collateral damage, and we must keep this minimal, but if it's meant to be, then we must follow through. Always keep others in mind as we move forward, and there will be times when an apology is appropriate, but we can have no shame and guilt for what is for our highest good. This is a fine line we walk daily, and our intentions must be true. Remember, the most important relationship we will ever have is with ourselves, so we must make hard decisions in our lives. Listen with your heart, not your wounded ego, and you will always be guided by the Divine.

## You Are A Limitless Being

Mankind has been taught from an early age that we must define ourselves, and be identified as something. In a twisted sense, this makes us tangible. In truth, defining ourselves limits us in many ways, as we feel the need to adhere to that definition. When we remain undefined, we maintain our limitless nature. Many believe we are defined by the 3D form that contains our Spirit self. That would mean that there is nothing beyond this incarnation. The Spirit will remain long after the body dies and will repeat incarnating in form. This proves that we cannot allow ourselves to be defined by the body, but rather the Spirit self. Opening up our belief that we are more than just a shell, we can allow ourselves to be the unlimited Being we truly are. There are endless possibilities to what we can be, so why limit ourselves to just the possibilities we can see? Evolution is going beyond our current state of being. Don't hold back your evolution just because you choose to limit yourself.

## Stepping Out Of The Box

Many of us have a very rigid routine that we follow daily, and we are quite happy within the comfort zone we have created. Routine is good, but all too often, we become mired down within the status quo we have created. Changing things up allows us to try different strategies, opening up new and wonderful opportunities to move beyond areas of our lives that we have become complacent within. Dare to be spontaneous. Choose to make one change within your life and take a step, even a small one, toward a new way of living beyond our accepted norm. This fresh approach will allow us to open ourselves to a realization that there is a better way than what we have allowed. Don't give into the ego's need for familiarity and limitations. We are limitless Beings who need to taste the freedom, brought by discovering that we are indeed more than we have allowed ourselves to be. Dare to step out of your comfort zone and become alive with a renewed sense of the self, without self-imposed limitations.

# Making Ourselves The Priority In Our Life

So many of us were raised to be there for everyone but ourselves. We learned from an early age to carry the burdens of others, taking on unhealthy roles in the midst of the family dysfunction, whether we had to be the hero, mediator, or scapegoat. Some of us took on more than a child's share of household chores and were little adults by the time we came out of grade school. As we grew older, our sense of duty rarely left us.

We became the "good soldier" in all areas of our adult life, always practical and on top of things, ready to lend a helping hand, and put more on our plate. Our focus was orientated on other people and their needs and expectations. We rarely said no when others had more responsibilities to add to our pile, and worked tirelessly, hiding our internal stress from ourselves and others. It never occurred to us that we really didn't need to live our lives like this as adults and that we have choices. No one ever told us that we could just get off the merry-go-round and actually start living, breathing, and be fully in the moment. It may be new to us that we could actually enjoy our lives and be free, instead of being driven on by the massive load of responsibilities that we took on.

For those who have always taken the role of the overly responsible good worker, it is time to learn to say no and learn to set healthy boundaries. Of course, it is convenient for others if we are always there to do more than our share, and they may protest if we stop over-giving. But truly, if we have built our lives around sacrificing ourselves for others, whether for their approval, to keep the peace, or to feel a sense of control, it's time to stop.

There are those of us who feel that if we don't do everything ourselves, it either doesn't get done at all or that no one does it a well as we do. And because these self-destructive patterns are so familiar, and usually passed down in the family line for generations, we don't realize how controlling we actually have become. While this sense of superiority may feel good to counter our low self-esteem, this is hardly a balanced, healthy way to live and engage with others. Nor are we allowing others to participate and be themselves. In fact, our being overly responsible leaves them feeling inferior and stifled.

There comes a point in our lives, when we simply cannot keep going on these self-destructive tracks, regardless of how engrained the patterns are. Our nervous system is frazzled by decades of overload and little self-care, our health is suffering, and our relationships are strained. Our own happiness and wellbeing doesn't even make it onto our priority list. We have created a life on the run, based on efficiency, where checking things off our lists is more important than feeling at home in ourselves, and embracing the gifts that life has been trying to offer to us.

But the Universe has ways of stopping us in our tracks when it's time to shift our focus back to ourselves, and come out of auto-pilot mode. It may take a health crisis, a natural disaster, the loss of a loved one, other some other life event to break us open enough to finally be willing to allow change, let go, and actually take care of all aspects of our self.

Self-love and making ourselves the highest priority in our life does not mean that we are selfish or abandoning others. We can still be there for them, with full attention, emotional availability, and support. But we don't empty our cup anymore to fill that of another. We don't take on responsibilities that are not ours to take. With healthy internal and external boundaries in place, our life suddenly has room for us, the precious being whose life this actually is.

Maybe it's the one-hour mediation, nap in the afternoon, or walk in the park that brings the space you need into your day. But it isn't just a matter of adding a little self-care routine to your already over-full day. What is needed is a fundamental change in mindset and perspective to actually give your self the priority in your life that you deserve and that will create space for your happiness.

# Learning Healthy External Boundaries

A healthy boundary to set for yourself is to no longer accept the pain someone else wants you to have. Simply reject their "gift." It's not yours, so it's not your responsibility to carry their pain. This is self-love and self-respect on the deepest level of unconditional love. Stop allowing them to control you. You deserve the inner peace that you'll feel once you've made up your mind to reject what is not for your highest good. They are responsible for their pain, as we are responsible for our own happiness. Change your mindset and set this boundary that says, "I love myself." Boundaries are set in place to let others know that it is not acceptable for you to be treated with anything but the respect you deserve. Their projection has nothing to do with you. Speak your truth. They may not like it, but do you honestly like their effort to make you feel small? Find your center and love yourself. Let the shame and guilt fall off. It's not yours to own. Give yourself the love they can't give you, and choose the love and inner peace you deserve.

## Safely Releasing Our Emotions

There will be times on your journey when you feel like your world is falling apart, you truly feel madness coursing through your soul, and you've reached that point when you absolutely feel the need to explode. Then allow yourself to release all that has been pent up inside, let it out till there is nothing left, but you crying the healing tears you need to shed lifetimes of trauma and pain. Find some place safe, and without projecting it onto others, where you can fully allow the rage, the anger, the frustration, the feeling, and the need to scream so the whole world can feel your pain, and let it out. When you are done releasing it all, go back within yourself and see how much you have let go and feel the space you have created inside that will now be filled with beautiful light. You need to know that you're okay and you're going to be okay. Be loving and compassionate with yourself. Treat yourself even if it's something small. Enjoy your sense of freedom but don't believe you are ever done, as there will always be more emotional healing work to do.

# The Damaging Effect Of Projections

When we project our emotions onto others, whether aware or subconsciously, we send that energy to them, normally being absorbed by an innocent being. All too often their response or reaction will be to feel small, beat down, and wondering what they did to deserve our wrath. How do we not project and wind up creating an unnecessary situation? We start by setting healthy internal boundaries that prevent our ego from acting out and forcing our emotional baggage onto the outside world. Having awareness, we catch ourselves and refrain from speaking in anger or blame, and stop our need to inflict our own pain and trauma onto others. We take full ownership of our own emotions, and make time to sit and feel, and get to the bottom of our triggers. We do the emotional healing work necessary to step out of the victim- perpetrator game, and into clarity from the heart.

## Learning Discernment of Energies

The energies of the planetary alignments affect our physical and emotional bodies. They also affect how we perceive the events and experiences in our immediate surroundings. At times, the day may seem weird and bizarre, almost surreal. Allow the time period to pass without judging it. What you may be feeling are the planetary energies bouncing off of each other, or perhaps the collective energy is strong at this time. The only way to truly know is through discernment of knowing your energy signature. To know your signature, one must take the inward journey to self-mastery and healing, knowing yourself deeply, trusting and believing in yourself. When we know our energy signature, we can tell what our emotion and energy is, and what is not. This will, undoubtedly, make the time period easier to navigate, without judging it and taking on whatever we feel by making it ours when it may not be. Get to know yourself and simplify your journey.

## Don't Lower Your Energy For Others

We can never allow ourselves to downplay our energy so another can be comfortable in our company. We must be true to ourselves, with honesty. How they see us is a reflection of their relationship with themselves, therefore, we can't take it personally. We are not responsible for the perceptions of others, nor are we responsible for their responses or reactions. To be quite honest, how another sees us is none of our business. Lowering our energy for the purpose of another is, in actuality, enabling them. It shows them they aren't accountable for what is theirs to own. It also allows them to maintain their sense of entitlement, believing we are at fault if we don't conform to their ways. We can no longer give our most sacred possession, our energy, to people-pleasing. We can no longer compromise our integrity and our authenticity just to appease another. Stand tall in your truth and never allow another to demand that you be someone other than who you have worked hard to become.

# From The Ashes Of The Old

All of us are muddling through these historic days, where the crumbling of the outdated patriarchal system, and the emerging of the new age of balance, higher consciousness, and diversity-within-unity are standing side by side. Many of us are being thrown into emotional upheavals, as old wounds resurface, and we are ushered into the next round of healing and personal evolution.

It is not always easy to keep a balance, and maintain our internal and external boundaries, as the world around us is acting out and going crazy. We are smack in the middle of an intense universal shift on our planet - a quantum leap that has been prophesized for eons. We must allow the old destructive ways within us and in the outer world to disintegrate. From the ashes of what no longer serves us, the new is emerging in its brightness. Trust that you are and will be okay through this journey into the unknown, as we are building the foundation for living from the heart.

As our own personal frequency is rising along with that of the Earth, we are urged to be patient, and allow the discomfort of the unknown, and our newfound rawness and vulnerability. We are prompted to purge and heal as much as we can at this time, but none of this is under our own direction or control. These are not only historically unprecedented times for our outer world, but also on a personal level, as we allow the Universe to help us get unstuck and evolve. The less we try to figure out what is happening to us, the better off we are. Trust.

## Knowing Your Own Energy Signature

Have you ever felt your true energy? Try this. Focus on your Christ Conscious Center located at your breastplate, where your ribs meet. Now focus on your Sacred Space just below your Sacral Chakra. Allow the energy to flow from your Sacred Space upward to your Christ Conscious Center, but don't try to force it because you cannot force energy. Close your eyes and feel it emanate from your lower chest. Just allow it to flow. We all have to know our own energy signature for many reasons and purposes. Relax and let the energy flow. Eventually you'll feel your energy at its core. Don't get frustrated if it takes time... it's a process. Trust yourself.

## Taking Time for Yourself

How do you perceive today as you unwind and finally allow yourself to relax? Was it another stressful day? Or did you have a couple of hours that were challenging? Did you allow it to consume you or were you able to work through it? If every day is hard and challenging for you, do you take some time for you? Or do you feel you have to power through, adding to the stress you already feel? Perhaps taking a few moments for yourself to find your center is all you need to end the cycle of allowing the stress to overtake you. Sometimes all we need is to stop, focus on our breathing, relax the physical body, and allow the stress to be released. We all have a happy place we go to. Take a moment to allow yourself to enjoy it in peace. This resets the mind and relaxes the body. Get up, get a beverage, and choose to allow some beauty in your day. That moment you take for yourself will bring the calm you need. You deserve it. Carrying stress causes dis-ease and cellular trauma. Release it and allow yourself to breathe.

## Going Within For Our Answers

As we are prompted to heal the depth of our inner world, we find that we don't have the answers. We don't know how to heal our traumas. We don't understand how to overcome the deep hurt inside. We cannot fathom how to let the past go and live fully in the present. This place of not knowing is actually golden. We are not filling the space with affirmations or spiritual surface advice that we may have read on social media. We are finally open to receiving answers from within, which is where our innate wisdom resides, and our evolution takes place. We have a tendency to feel disconnected, exist within the limits of the 3D world of our body, and forget that our Spirit is of the Divine and possesses incredible knowledge. We don't remember that we are firmly embedded in the etheric wisdom of our ancestors, guides, and higher dimensional team. When we ask the Divine Mother and Father, and our Spirit and guides, to show us how to stop living in the past, and perpetuating our wounds, we invite the most capable help on our journey. We have stopped looking in the outer world for spiritual cookie cutter answers that will likely not move us forward, given the intricacies of our personal experiences and inner environment. We are learning to trust ourselves and allow our answers to come from within.

## **Collateral Beauty**

There is always a period of excruciating vulnerability following any traumatic experience. The norm we became accustomed to is no longer, nor shall it ever be again. This is a new phase of existence, normally feeling the extreme ranges of emotions. After an experience involving loss or trauma, we enter a period of mourning. It is during this time that we incur a quantum leap in our evolution. During our time of grief, we release more than just that experience and the emotions associated with it. We are, in fact, releasing all that has come to the surface that can no longer be a part of our lives. This brings an emotional clearing en masse, making room for what will serve our highest good. This, in part, is what is referred to as collateral beauty. Whether we can see that there is beauty in any period of darkness or not, we will come to a place of acceptance, and furthermore, a new balance within. Honoring what we feel, with patience, compassion, and trust, allows us to naturally enter the new life that is meant for us.

## Shift Your Perspective

There are always many ways to do something. Sometimes we simply need to see from a different perspective. If we keep trying to do the same things the same way, it becomes an exercise in futility. We can always figure out how not to do something, which will inevitably lead us to success. Don't give up just because it's not working right. Find a different way. Be open to the probability that the answer lies in a unique approach. Every inventor had to try other options in order to find the right combination. When frustration sets in, walk away for a bit, breathe, and readjust your thinking. Find your patience, become the observer, and open your mind to new and fresh ideas. This is how we learn. Don't allow your perceived limitations to be your block, stopping you from finding a solution. Oftentimes, we miss the obvious by believing the answer is beyond our focus. Trust yourself, and know you can. We aren't failing until we have totally given up. There is always a better way.

## Expanding Into The Unknown

Two of mankind's most dominant fears are of the darkness and the unknown. We have been taught since childhood that they are not only similar, but one in the same. The darkness represents what we cannot see, touch, or understand, and therefore we fear it. The unknown is simply that which is temporarily misunderstood. We fear what we cannot understand. How are we going to expand ourselves if we never allow ourselves to go into the unknown, bringing us understanding? This is a huge block on our journey that stops us dead in our tracks. One of our purposes - yes, we have many - is to learn. That means going right into what we don't know or understand. The darkness is a visual perception linked to our fear center... the ego. You have all you need already within you. Your courage, strength, drive, and desire are for you to find in what is believed by many to be our darkness. Always and in all ways, trust and believe in yourself. This is the only way to discover yourself and all your untapped potential, allowing you to be your authentic self.

# The Futility Of Forcing Our Agenda

When we have a personal agenda, we are not open to receiving guidance from the Divine, nor are we as connected to our intuition and gut feelings. Our expectation or attachment to a desired outcome keeps our focus and awareness narrowed to getting what we want – usually at the cost of our discernment and boundaries. We manipulate our own perception, blinding ourselves to reality, and ignoring our inner guidance system. This comes at a price, whether we get what we want or not, as this kind of self-abandonment and distractedness will compromise being centered and living from the heart. When we try to control our lives, we are automatically out of sync with the flow of the Universe, and unable to receive. This sense of separateness causes us stress and agony at all levels. If we believe that getting what we want is the antidote to our internal pain, we are increasing our sense of lack, entitlement, and unhappiness. Yet, surrender is the solution to our struggle, not forcing our agenda. Letting go of what we thought we needed so desperately, and trusting that we will be provided for, is what will bring us back to the moment, and open the connection with our own self and the Divine.

# Coming Out Of Victim Mode

Wanting to heal from any kind of abuse takes more than just saying, "I want to heal." There must be an action behind the words of intent. The words we choose will carry much weight in whether we actually heal from it or not. The first step to any healing is forgiveness of others and the self. We forgive because we deserve inner peace, not because they are deserving. Next, stop saying, "I am a victim of abuse." This actually keeps us locked into the victim mentality and owning the title of victim. Choose to say, "I am a survivor of abuse." This takes away ownership of being a victim, and states that you survived it and are coming out of being a victim. This puts us past the stage that we have outgrown, as we are no longer holding onto the pain and trauma that keeps us in the past. Bringing yourself back to the moment, the present, signifies a desire to move beyond a time that no longer exists. It's more valuable to you to hold onto the reality you currently live, rather than perpetuating the pain, holding onto it. Staying locked into being a victim will block you from actually healing.

# When Others Bring Drama Into Our Lives

No matter how hard we attempt to maintain a drama free existence, there will always be those who will bring it into our lives. So, how do we coexist with those who thrive from their need to share drama? Quite simply, by setting healthy boundaries, without becoming threatening or creating conflict above what they bring. Indeed, this will not always be an easy task, but we cannot allow ourselves to get caught up in their lifestyle, or allow it to affect our life and wellbeing. Speak your truth from the heart and don't concern yourself with their reaction or response, which is a reflection of their relationship with themselves and where they are on their journey. We don't have to accept the energy they project, as we need to protect our own energy field. Sometimes, it may signify the need to decide whether our shared journey should come to an end, but that will depend on how they react to our boundaries. Not everyone is meant to be in our lives long-term. Regardless, give them love and forgiveness, and allow the healing process to begin.

## Revisiting Old Wounds

There are times, when we revert to how small and ashamed we felt about ourselves due to the projections of others. We feel rotten to the core and utterly worthless. An old need to punish ourselves and martyr our time and energy re-arises, as if we hadn't done years of inner healing work to rebuild our self-esteem and love ourselves fiercely back to life. These are layers, my friend. You are not going back. You are revisiting the same old wounds, now ready to let go a bit more of what crushed your soul and made you feel lower than the stones. You are not this, nor were you ever.

These were violent projections, flung your way by wounded people who could not love themselves and preyed on those they perceived as weaker. This is on them. It had nothing to do with you, then, nor does it now. You are not who you were told to be, even if those projecting this onto you were your parents or caregivers. Trust that they could not see you in their blinding rage. It wasn't about you. This terrible bundle of soul crushing pain has been passed down from one generation to the next. You were forced to be the recipient, against your will, but you do not need to own and carry this toxic package any longer.

Stand firm in who you know yourself to be, flaws and all, with complete acceptance, and no longer accept what is not yours to carry. Reframe your experiences and free yourself from other people's toxic projections. It is your birthright to be you, and no one has the right to make you feel ashamed for being you.

Shine your light brightly, own who you are, and stand tall in who you have become. This is who you are. Create a loving space for yourself within your own heart, and you will never feel an outcast or unloved ever again.

## Allowing Changes In Our Relationships

Dynamics within any relationship are constantly changing because we, as individuals, are in a state of constant change. We aren't always going to be able to hear each other, but that doesn't mean there has to be conflict within the dynamic. Allow the fact and reality of these changes, and keep up with them. We learn to adapt to any changes, whether within ourselves or with others. Struggle doesn't have to be an obstacle if we learn to flow with the moment. What is truly important to remember is that everyone is always going through something in their lives, not just us. We're not always going to have understanding, and there will be frustrations that will come forward. Center back into the heart space, the Spirit self, with the understanding that all is temporary, and this too shall pass. Remember the love that is shared within the dynamic and never lose sight of that.

## The Right To Choose

As we evolve, our frequency also evolves, becoming greater. Whether we have awareness or not, it does affect others around us, especially those we are close to. This means we are changing and growing. Each of us grows in different ways and measures, depending on who is in charge, the Spirit self, or the 3D self. The Spirit will always evolve in a manner for our highest good, while the 3D self may not always follow in this way. We all have choice, our free will, and oftentimes the 3D self will not have awareness of the Spirit self and will only follow a 3D regimen. It's sometimes easier for the 3D self to just be content in the bit of happiness they have found, rather than follow their Divine purpose, and that's okay. We all have a right to the life we choose, and this choice is not open to commentary when we respect the choices of others. We all will be affected by these choices and, unfortunately, many will be misunderstood with their reaction or response. Don't assume silence is rejection, as it may be respect for another's choices and boundaries they have set.

# Actions Speak Louder Than Words

There have been many times in our lives when we can't find the words to express what we feel. There is no guilt or shame in that. Our actions, or lack thereof, will become the exact expression we lack verbally. Believing we have chosen to not decide, our actions betray us, signifying our choice. This is normally an unconscious response from our cellular self. Regardless, we are projecting the exact expression that we don't have the temporary vocabulary for. Empathically, others will sense this with awareness and realization of the fact that actions will always speak louder than words. In the end, we have expressed ourselves openly and honestly without actually realizing it. We may have the intention to hide our true feelings, but our actions, put forth by the cellular self, show our truth. We can't hide from others how we truly feel, but we can fool ourselves into believing that ignoring our emotions will simply make them disappear.

## Honoring Another's Truth

Our perception has the ability to hold others guilty of nothing more than not having all the facts. Our ego has stepped in as judge and jury, without so much as an interest in what is in the hearts of others. Before we condemn others, at least listen to their truth without our biased ego interfering. This will save much unnecessary heartache and broken relationships. They deserve to speak their truth and be heard, just as much as you deserve to hear their truth. Don't lock another out of your heart without knowing all the facts. If you truly love them, then hear them out with the respect all are deserving of. Perhaps you'll see your perception was wrong. Perhaps they will choose to take the same mentality you chose, and the relationship is broken. Before you decide they are in the wrong, stop your thought process and consider your own part in it all. Are you the innocent one? Are they? Is there really a guilty party? What is the honest truth? At least allow their truth to be spoken before judging them based on what you don't know.

## Embracing our Emotions

Creating an illusion that all is well and that nothing is wrong in our lives, is disguising the truth and a denial of our reality. I do know there are those whose lives are "perfect." They had amazing childhoods, and all is in some semblance of balance. They live this life on the surface, never desiring to touch anything that would upset their bubble. We can choose to live this kind of life and deny ourselves many wonderful opportunities to grow. We all have free will. No one has ever had a "perfect life" simply because we are human beings with emotions and feelings. If nothing has ever bothered us, then I truly believe that being has never been in touch with their emotional self. I lived for a few years with a belief that I was happy because I bought into the spiritual belief that meditation would bring me inner peace. Then reality hit me head on, and I realized that all I did was ignore my emotional self, and I began damage control, which took years. Allow yourself to feel. Be honest with yourself. If it hurts, then it's real. I learned to heal my emotional trauma and be fully alive.

## Unlearning Perfectionism

We will never be able to know what should be done in every situation, especially if we have no point of reference from a previous experience. An unfortunate human condition is to believe we should have known what the appropriate response or reaction was. Our wounded ego has just led us to believe that we are omnipotent, and did not correctly measure our response or reaction. This is an incredibly self-sabotaging effort, bringing undue shame and guilt to the self. Was our attempt sufficient and proper? Perhaps we'll never know the answer, and our ego will make sure we punish ourselves through our guilt and shame. To equalize this internal struggle, give love and compassion to the self, with forgiveness and grace. Help heal and balance the ego and bring it this new understanding, allowing it and yourself to evolve through changing this old pattern and belief of perfectionism. This is vulnerability, and the only state in which we can learn, heal, and grow.

## Being The Observer

It's not hard to become so locked into the perception of our own deep pain and wounds that we can no longer see beyond that pain, and it becomes all that exists, all consuming, and all encompassing. We perpetuate a painful experience through the eyes of our own need to demand justice from others, when in truth, if we look back upon it, we can see deeper into our self from the eyes of the observer. The observer has the ability to see a much different perspective. Time and again, as I personally reflect on an experience as the observer, I see the truth beyond my own pain, with the realization that I was the one in the wrong. All we can do with that realization is ask forgiveness and own what was ours. We can give ourselves at that love, with the permission to change our old beliefs and our need to blame someone for our pain. There is no need for blame, shame, or guilt to be cast upon ourselves from then, or now, or others involved. We can't make our yesterdays right. We can, however, heal, learn, and grow from our newfound perspective, with love and grace, and make the changes within the self to allow forward and upward movement.

## Moving On From The Past

Many of us haven't discovered that we can be more than we were yesterday. We tend to see ourselves as we have always been, not who we can be and are. Stuck inside our former selves, locked within our comfort zone, we create a prison, unable to move forward and evolve. Humanity has much untapped potential. If we only trusted and believed in ourselves just a little more each day, we would realize our potentials fully. Sadly, many of us can't see beyond the pains and traumas of our yesterdays, perpetuating what we so desperately long to be gone. What we focus on becomes our lives. When all we feel is pain from a time that no longer exists, we become consumed by that. Somehow, we must rise above those pains. All it takes is a desire and action to make it happen. That change won't manifest until we're ready for change. When we finally decide we're tired of a painful existence is the day we will make the change. Not until. How many times have you admitted to yourself that you can't continue like this anymore? Then why keep living it?

## Balancing Our Darkness

Oftentimes, when we are experiencing an emotional period that we can't define, we are facing something within our darkness we haven't been able to touch before. We can't define it because we have no reference point for where the emotional upheaval is located within. This is perfectly natural, and we should simply allow it to exist and honor it, just as we would any recognizable emotional pitfall. This is a natural process of our darkness that is also evolving, as we are within our light. Yes, our darkness has to maintain a balance within, so that it does, in fact, evolve, the same as our light. Our frequency elevates often without our recognition, which is also a natural occurrence. It just kind of sneaks up on us, simply because we have much on our plate. There's nothing wrong with us, rather, the Universe is gently giving us a nudge forward, and we don't need to understand it. Give gratitude and allow it to flow, loving yourself with compassion, as you normally would during any emotionally charged period. You're okay, and you're going to be okay.

## Don't Ever Lose Hope

Beauty will always exist within the darkness, pains, and traumas we experience. All it takes is a split second of awareness and recognition of that beauty to turn our lives around. That short time can and will bring us out of the darkness we live within to bring us on the path to healing. It takes the same energy to see light as it takes to exist in darkness. The same energy. You have the ability to choose between them. Your Spirit is longing to feel something other than the harshness of life many of us can become stuck within. When we become overwhelmed by our pain, we can still feel something different. Perhaps the gesture of a smile from a stranger, a song that takes us back to a better time, or even a funny meme on social media. Anything that can bring a smile, no matter how temporary, is enough to bring us out of the fog we have been in.

Indeed, many of us have chosen at some point in our lives to live in solitude. I personally went into hermit mode for about six years, and I don't regret one minute of my choice. I wasn't in a place to be available to others as my emotional healing journey dictated this need. I guarantee few will have understanding, and probably will feel as if they have done something wrong. Again, I personally experienced this, especially when I entered the dreaded Dark Night of the Soul. I went deep within my darkness, not understanding what was happening. I tried reassuring the people in my life that it wasn't about them. My final recourse was to tell them just let me go through what I need to and honor my need to be alone.

I tend to separate myself from others when I'm deep in processing. I don't want to project my woundedness upon the undeserving as my emotions become quite intense. Neha and I have no problem saying we need downtime. There is always the offer to talk, but there is always the respect of the healing process. It may take hours, it may take days, but we always honor the needs of each other. The world could use a lot more of this honor and respect. Taking the processing deep, we enter into the unknown depths of our pains farther than any layer of healing before. Even through all of this, I have the ability to see beauty. Something else we need within our darkness is the ability to give gratitude.

Many times when I'm crying deeply, painfully releasing, I will give thanks. How is it possible to be deep in pain and still be able to give thanks? By simply stepping back into the heart space, if even for just that moment. We become so mired down by the weight of our emotions that pain is all we see and feel. This momentary visit to our heart allows us to remember there is beauty within all we endure. It prompts us to regain our strength and courage. Personally, the beauty of knowing I can trust so deeply in the Divine is what keeps me going through all I have ever experienced. Indeed, I know I must process what has been brought, but the love I feel when I touch the trust I possess always reminds me that this is temporary.

I know deep within my heart that I'm being watched over, protected, and in the loving embrace of the Highest Being. This is trust. I embrace the love I feel from within myself, and I know I'm okay, and I'm going to be okay. This is truly one of the most beautiful experiences I have ever had. I know, without a shadow of a doubt, that I'll never feel that sudden stop as I spiral downward within the darkness my life has become. How can this affect my healing process? Just the knowing that I'm so very loved will bring me back to my heart space. The warmth that takes over my entire being has a profound effect, and allows me to understand that I'm never alone.

I'm able to eventually release what I must to heal the pains and traumas that I am feeling. It's kind of like an open window in a house that has been closed up for days. I realize at this point that I have gone through the darkness and found the light I need. I have come back to me and into my heart space again. I know that releasing is all that's left, and all will be right within my world once again. It's imperative that we do not lose hope. Choosing to see even a glimmer of beauty will keep that hope alive within. I know at this time that this too shall pass. I have endured my darkness and I'm on my way to the other side of my pain, until the next layer comes to be healed. This is how beauty will change everything. Don't ever lose sight of your heart. Don't ever lose hope.

## Cleansing Your Space

Leaving the comfort of our immediate environment will have an amazing effect upon our energetic field, as well as our mental state. We become so accustomed to our own energetic space that we don't realize this is where we process and heal. When we process deeply, we tend to "throw" the energy we are trying to contend with, filling our living space with, at times, an inordinate amount of unwanted energy. We keep surrounding ourselves with the energy we have been trying to release. We need to energetically cleanse our living environment. There are many ways to cleanse energy, so find one that resonates with you. We use copal resin and a charcoal tablet to cleanse our space, normally every day. Getting outside of all that unwanted energy allows the physical body to refresh its auric field. Offer that energy to Mother Earth to be transmuted back into a useful energy for her. She will gladly absorb your excess to strengthen her energy field to fight all that humanity is doing to harm her. Water is another awesome way to cleanse your auric field. When showering or bathing ask the water to cleanse your field. I believe many of you will be surprised at the results. When we have sufficiently cleansed our energy, coming home will feel very different energetically. It's lighter and brighter, and we have just returned with a renewed perspective, ready to face the next round of processing. Another layer of healing is complete, and we have just evolved again.

## Experiencing Beyond Our Survival Mode

The power of a change in perspective is unfathomable when we are operating from a limited mindset. Our perception at any given moment is jaded by what we have been taught, and what has been projected onto us. Experiencing traumatic events earlier in life, our minds are locked into an incredibly limited perspective. Our perception of ourselves and everything around us shrank to the single focal point of fear for our own safety, and concern for our familiar comfort. We became self-centered from a narrow, survival-oriented viewpoint that reflects the pain and loss of self we experienced. But we have always had the power to heal and break out of the limitations that we placed upon ourselves. When we become aware of negative, self-centered thoughts or actions, we have a chance to allow a change in perspective. We can let go of our mental control and attempts to manipulate our perceptions, and allow life to come to us, widening our horizons. With self-love and compassion, we can allow the necessary emotional healing to take place so that we can live and thrive, and not just continue existing in the box of survival mode. Let down your walls. There is a beautiful, magical world within and all around you. Give yourself permission to explore and see with different eyes.

## Our Internal Dance Of Light And Dark

Life takes on a whole new quality when we know that the reality of our life will always be a dance of light and darkness. On this plane of existence, there is no such thing as only light, only love, or everlasting joy and happiness. As such, conflict is needed, in whatever form and to whatever degree, so that we can learn our soul lessons and evolve. Because duality is so pronounced on Earth, and the atmosphere so heavy, many souls incarnate here to be able to heal their ancient wounds and make great progress on their evolutionary journey. Our healing journey is not about managing our internal turmoil to the point of repression, but allowing ourselves to dive deeply into our own darkness or shadow world, and exploring all sides of who we are. We then have choice, and can use our darkness to fuel our light, instead of letting it take over, making a mess of our lives through unconscious patterns and behaviors. When we can embrace our own personal shadows as much as our inherent Divine light, we have the ability to find balance and wholeness through healing the wounded consciousnesses within, and creating right order and healthy boundaries. We are able to accept the whole of ourselves, not just the parts that we like best and find more acceptable than others, and lift all parts of ourselves back into the love in our hearts.

# Gary's Book: An Awakening Perspective
# My Journey To Conscious Evolution

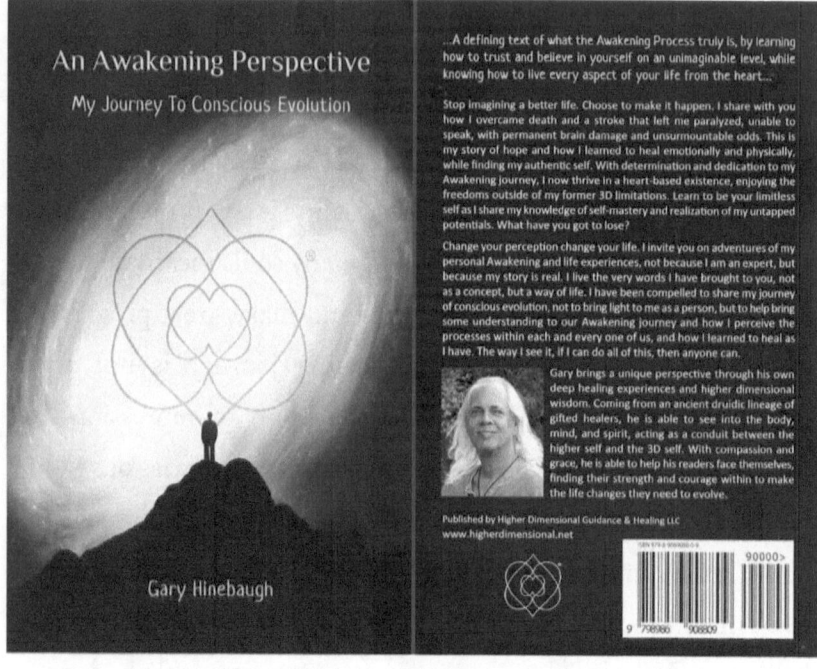

If you ever thought that there is more to life than what you know, this book is for you. Gary gives deep insight into the many processes of the awakening journey from his own experiences. Having to reach deep within himself to overcome a paralyzing stroke and near impossible odds, he discovered within himself the will and strength to break down the barriers of human limitations, and heal his physical and emotional self. Being thrown into circumstances, with no choice but to trust the Divine implicitly, facilitated a depth of connection with the Higher Dimensions that allows him to access universal wisdom and higher dimensional knowledge.

In this book, he helps his readers remember their authentic self and unbecome what was projected onto them since childhood. Bringing a fresh perspective in line with the timeless messages of ancient mystery schools, druids, shamans, and sages, Gary assists the reader with becoming unstuck, changing harmful mental and emotional patterns, and accelerating their evolution.

Carried along by the encouragement of his words, loving energy, humor, and compassionate tone, it will be hard to put this book down. An exciting journey of self-discovery and increased awareness – with countless aha-moments – awaits you within its pages, welcoming you home to your self and the inner freedom that you have been yearning for. Relearn to trust and believe in yourself, and reclaim your Divine sovereignty!

To purchase your copy, go to our website:

https://higherdimensional.net